The Value-Able Child

Teaching Values at Home and School

Kathleen Long Bostrom

Good Year Books

An Imprint of Addison-Wesley Educational Publishers, Inc.

To Laura, my very able editor, my dearly valued friend

 Good Year Books are available for most basic curriculum subjects plus many enrichment areas. For more Good Year Books, contact your local bookseller or educational dealer. For a complete catalog with information about other Good Year Books, please write to

Good Year Books

1900 East Lake Avenue

Glenview, Illinois 60025

Design: Nancy Rudd

Illustration: Paige Billin-Frye and Nancy Rudd

Copyright © 1999 Good Year Books, an imprint of Addison-Wesley Educational Publishers, Inc.

All Rights Reserved.

Printed in the United States of America.

ISBN 0-673-58639-1

1 2 3 4 5 6 7 8 9 - ML - 06 05 04 03 02 01 00 99

Table of Contents

Introduction

They start arriving in November, filling my mailbox with paper and my heart with memories of friends near and distant. I look forward to them, although sitting down to write my own seems to take more effort than it should. I'm referring to the annual holiday letters that have become a staple over the last few years, replacing the signature-only cards of long ago.

The letters of my friends with children are chock-full of all of the many accomplishments of their offspring: the sports in which they are involved, the musical instruments they play, the academic awards they've earned, the clubs they are in. These activities and ambitions define our children as they are growing up. Every year I am struck by these letters, and the amount of importance we all place on what our children "do" rather than "who" they actually are. Rarely does anyone ever write that "Sarah has a good, kind heart," or "Tom is an expert at being a true friend," or "Lily sets a great example of cooperation in our family."

In a society where economic success and academic achievements seem to be the only measures of a person's worth, it is ever more important to get back to stressing values. What are values? Values are the intrinsic principles that give life real meaning. Values are the intangible resources that give a person true worth. Values are what the word itself implies—that which brings value to our existence as human beings. The ability we have to define and activate values in our lives sets us apart from all other living species. Yet values do not just happen. They are taught, and they can be learned from the moment a child enters the world. If kindness is displayed in the home, children will learn kindness. If honesty is practiced, it will become a habit. If forgiveness is given, it will be returned. Children learn from what we do, what we say, and how we live.

"We grow morally as a consequence of learning how to be with others, how to behave in this world, a learning prompted by taking to heart what we have seen and heard," wrote Robert Coles, a Pulitzer prize-winning author and recognized expert on the moral and spiritual development of children. (*Time,* Jan. 20, 1997, p. 48) Parents, teachers, athletes, celebrities—all adults are role models for younger generations. But there are other powerful forces in the lives of our children. Television, electronic video games, and movies also have an impact on the values our children learn. That is why it is essential for teachers and parents not just to teach but to live out the values we hold to be of greatest worth.

And what could be more valuable to our lives, to our society, to the world, than our children? How do we encourage them to become "value-able" people— people who are able to live by the values that are necessary for a healthy and happy life?

The Value-Able Child: Teaching Values at Home and School is designed to help teachers and parents work as a team both to teach values to children and to assist them in activating these values in their daily living, to teach them to be "value-able" people, a gift that will sustain them their whole lives. In the words of author William J. Bennett, "We must not permit our disputes over thorny political questions to obscure the obligation we have to offer instruction to all our young people in the area in which we have, as a society, reached a consensus: namely, on the importance of good character, and on some of its pervasive particulars." (*The Book of Virtues,* p. 13)

As we work together to teach our children the values that will enable them to be "value-able," we may just find ourselves becoming more intentional about the values by which we choose to live. We could start with those annual holiday letters!

Values Defined

What are values? Let's take a look at how *values* is defined by others:

■ "A true and universally accepted value is one that produces behavior that is beneficial both to the practitioner and to those on whom it is practiced." (*Teaching Your Children Values,* by Linda and Richard Eyre, p. 27)

■ "Your values are the guiding principles or ideals that govern your daily actions by prioritizing the competing interests in your life. Our values are the freely chosen precepts that help guide our daily decisions and actions, thereby giving increased meaning and direction to our lives. Values are cherished worthwhile beliefs that enable us to affirm and respect ourselves and others." (*Dr. Mom's Parenting Guide,* by Marianne Neifert, M.D., p. 167)

■ ". . . a set of fundamental beliefs that we hold." (*Helping Children Choose,* by George M. Schuncke and Suzanne Lowell Krogh, p. 3)

Values are those basic, foundational beliefs that help us know right from wrong, that give balance and meaning to life, that enable us to live in community with one another. Values enhance our own lives and the lives of others. We are not born with a specific set of values imprinted upon our psyche: values are learned by observation and through interaction, and they are learned by living them.

Why Teach Values?

Think of values as being the roots of a tree. The roots anchor the tree to the ground, pulling nutrients and water from the soil. The roots are essential to the health of the tree. They allow the rest of the plant to grow and flourish. The roots are often hidden completely from view, but without them, the tree will die.

How to Use This Book

The Value-Able Child uses a team approach to teaching values. Teachers, parents, and children are all involved in the learning experience. To allow for this holistic approach, information and activities are provided for use in school, at home, and in the community.

Why Teach Values at School?

Robert Coles states that "In elementary school, maybe as never before or ever afterwards, the child becomes an intensely moral creature, quite interested in figuring out the reasons of this world—how and why things work, but also, how and why he or she should behave in various situations." (*Time,* Jan. 20, 1997, p. 50)

According to recent statistics, there will be 54.6 million school-age children by the year 2006. (*Publisher's Weekly,* Jan. 27, 1997, p. 32) This is an increase of 3 million children from the 1996 enrollment.

It only makes sense then that schools assist parents in teaching values to children. Many children spend a significant amount of their daytime hours in a school setting. School is a place where the values will come into play. And children learn best in settings where there is interaction with others—an inevitable occurrence in schools.

Teachers and all educators must be intentional about teaching values to students, including modeling the values in their everyday interactions with the students. Indeed, modeling may be the most effective mode of teaching; therefore, it must be consistent and sincere.

Use for Home-Schooling

For those parents who choose to home-school their children, the same principles apply. If you are both parent and teacher, it is essential that in both capacities, you model values for your children. *The Value-Able Child* can be used in home-schools, and in fact, is an important resource in reinforcing ways of teaching children values that they will need not only at home, but everywhere.

Why Teach Values at Home?

For better or for worse, parents and family are the greatest influence in a child's life. From the very first moments a parent holds a child in his or her arms, the child begins to learn. Can I trust? Am I lovable? What is important in life?

Too often, parents are not properly prepared for the job of raising children. But parents and teachers work together, promoting similar values and thus providing a consistent teaching of these values. Children can share what they've learned at school with their families, even as they bring to school the values they've learned at home. The more that parents and families are aware of what is being taught in the schools, the more they can reinforce the implementation of the values being taught.

Why Include the Community?

Values are not just for personal use. In order for values to truly be defined and implemented, they need to be shared with others. As children grow, they become more exposed to the outside world. They need to know from an early age that their behavior and assistance can help others beyond their immediate circles. Involvement in community outreach helps build a child's self-esteem and leads to the cultivation of a healthier society.

"The future is in the hands of those who can give tomorrow's generations valid reasons to live and hope." (Teilhard de Chardin, theologian and philosopher) This is our job—as parents, teachers, educators, adults.

So let's join hands together!

Chapter Contents

The Value-Able Child consists of ten chapters, each chapter based on one of ten values: Cooperation, Courage, Friendship, Honesty, Kindness, Loyalty, Respect, Self-Control, Sharing, Tolerance. The chapters can be used in any order. Each chapter includes eight sections:

Before You Begin: an introduction for the parent/teacher/group leader that defines and explains the value and why it is important for children to learn.

To the Family: a list of suggestions for reinforcing the value at home, with all family members. Although designed for the teacher to send home to parents, parents who have purchased the book themselves will find it a great resource full of valuable tips.

Let's Get Started!: a brief introduction written as a script to share with the children in preparation for the study of each value.

Fingerplay: a separate fingerplay for each value, sung to the tune of a popular nursery rhyme. The fingerplays give the children a fun and easy way to remember the different values.

Time for a Story!: an engaging read-aloud story based on each value. Following the story are discussion questions that encourages the children to think for themselves about the value and the consequences of their actions in relation to the value.

1-2-3 Activities!: three activities to reinforce the chapter's value. An introduction to each activity explains how it is done and what supplies are needed. Reproducible Activity Sheets provide a way for children to participate in hands-on learning.

Community Connections: suggestions for promoting each value within the entire community. See what other ideas you can think of!

Reading List: a list of good books for young children that exemplify the various values. These lists are by no means exhaustive! Check your local library for other books that appeal to children. Reading with children is a wonderful way to open the door for discussions about values.

Home-School Tips

Many parents choose to teach their children at home, instead of sending them to a public or private school. *The Value-Able Child* can be used in a home-school setting. When particular activities or suggestions are geared for classroom use with a multiple number of children, you will find a small "Home-School" icon with helpful tips for adapting that portion of the book for home-school use.

Appendix

The Appendix includes suggestions for ongoing group projects that give an overall view of the ten values. The projects are titled "A Tree of Values," "A Living Rainbow," "Hand-in-Hand Around the World," "Wall of Fame," "WANTED Posters," and "Student Journal." Also in the Appendix is a reproducible journal page and an Award Certificate. The Award Certificate is given to all students who complete the program.

"The Values Song"

"The Values Song" helps us remember the names of the ten values we are learning. It can be sung at the beginning of each lesson on values.

"The Values Song"

Sung to the tune of "Ten Little Indians"

One and two and three good values,
Four and five and six good values,
Seven and eight and nine good values,
Ten good ways to live.
Kindness, Honesty, and Friendship,
Self-Control, Cooperation,
Courage, Loyalty, and Sharing,
Tolerance, Respect.
We can learn the ten good values,
Try to live the way they teach us;
As we do, we'll all become
The best that we can be!

CHAPTER 1

Cooperation

Before You Begin

1, 2, 3—Teamwork!

The Reeve family has a tradition. Whenever they have a problem that needs to be solved, a job to do, or an activity to plan, they join together in a circle. Together, they count off, "One, two, three—TEAMWORK!" As they say the word *teamwork,* they each put one hand in the middle of the circle, thumbs up. This is their way of reminding one another that they are a family where cooperation is cherished. Everyone works together whenever possible.

So much of life promotes competition: sports, grades, jobs, even the seeking of a parent's undivided attention. Often the goal is to "win" more than it is to do one's best or to have a good time. The belief that you have to be better than somebody else does little to encourage cooperation. Competition is fine in some situations, but it's not the best way to solve most problems. And competition is the source of a great deal of sibling rivalry, vocational dissatisfaction, stress, and depression.

Check your bookstore or library for books that teach games based on cooperation rather than competition, such as *The Cooperative Sports and Games Book: Challenge without Competition* by Terry Orlick and *Energizers and Other Great Cooperative Activities for All Ages* by Carol Apacki. Seek methods of promoting cooperation in daily tasks, problem solving, and activities. If you can't find good resources, invite the children to come up with ideas of their own.

Cooperation doesn't just happen. It takes willingness on all sides. As children discover ways to cooperate with one another, they will find that working toward a solution can be as exciting and challenging as finding a good solution where everybody is a winner.

Why not borrow a good idea and adopt the tradition of the Reeve family? "1, 2, 3—Teamwork!" is a great motto for everyone to live by.

Dear Family:

Imagine a family where everyone worked together, where chores were tackled with enthusiasm, where children looked for ways to help each other out. Sound impossible? It might not be—if that's what you expect all the time.

Cooperation among family members is not an unreachable dream. Cooperation may not be the order of every day, but it can be incorporated into family life in subtle and obvious ways. Here are a few suggestions.

■ Encourage children to work out their problems together.

Parents have a tendency to want to referee their children's fights. This is necessary when one child has the potential to physically injure a sibling. Whenever possible, however, allow children to work out their problems without your interference. Help them set guidelines: everyone gets five minutes to state his or her feelings and the problem; there is no physical contact; the solution must be agreeable to all. Children gain a sense of accomplishment in solving their problems, and they will be better equipped to deal with other people if they practice cooperation at home.

■ Join resources to buy or make a gift.

Kelsey's birthday is coming up. More than anything, she wants a pet parakeet. But buying the pet and all the equipment adds up! Time to join resources.

One child can buy the parakeet. Another may buy the seed or a perch. Parents can pitch in for the cage. By pooling your resources, Kelsey gets the one gift she really wants and all the family members enjoy the satisfaction of cooperating together to help Kelsey's dream come true.

■ Work together for a common goal.

The weather this weekend is supposed to be sunny and clear. Everyone wants to spend the day at the local amusement park. But Mom and Dad have worked all week, and the house is a mess. Saturday is usually the day to catch up on all the chores that are left during the week.

Now's the time to say, "If we all work together on Friday evening to clean the house, we'll have time to go to the park on Saturday." Let each family member sign up for a chore. Even three-year-old Jeremy can take an old sock and dust the baseboards. Cooperation allows everybody to have some time for fun. And it teaches children that their efforts are necessary to keep the household running smoothly.

■ Avoid questions that promote competition among family members.

It's report card day. When the children arrive home, the first question you want to ask is, "What grades did you get?" But if one child is prone to getting good grades and another is not, this question instantly becomes a source of unhealthy competition between the children. The same is true for questions such as, "Did you win the game?"

Try these alternative questions: "Tell me about your report card. Which class did you enjoy this semester?" and "Did you have a good time at the soccer game?" Children's worth should come not because they achieve, although it is fine to celebrate their success. Just be careful not to make "winning" the ultimate goal.

■ Thank everyone when they cooperate.

It's easy to get angry when children refuse to cooperate. Yet do we thank them for the times when they do work together? Positive encouragement always goes further than negative reactions. Even though you may see cooperation as a nonnegotiable component of family life, it never hurts to thank children when they do what is expected of them.

Let home be a place of cooperative effort, where teamwork is rewarded and where time is given to work through problems together. A happy family is a team effort. And every member of the team is just as important as anyone else.

Let's Get Started!

Would you like to join me in a Cooperation Celebration?

That's a mouthful, isn't it? "Cooperation Celebration." It sounds as if I'm inviting you to a party, and I am. What do we need to have a party?

- We need snacks.
- We need games.
- We need music.

What else?

People! That's right, people. We can't have a party with just one person. That wouldn't be much fun. It takes a bunch of people to have a party. That's why you are all invited to the Cooperation Celebration.

What are we celebrating? Cooperation! We need to cooperate with one another in order to have a successful party. We need to decide together which games we will play, what snacks we will eat, and what music to have. A Cooperation Celebration won't work unless we all cooperate as a team.

After we learn our fingerplay on cooperation, we'll divide into teams: the Snack Squad, the Game Group, and the Song Throng. We'll all be part of the Cleanup Crew.

I can't wait for the Cooperation Celebration! I'm so glad you're all going to join me. I know we're going to have a great time.

HOME SCHOOL TIP

Instead of dividing into teams, you and your child(ren) can be one team and cooperate together in deciding on snacks, games, and songs.

Fingerplay

TO THE TUNE OF
"Ring Around the Rosey"

(Stand in a circle.)

Join the celebration
(Hold hands out to side.)

Of cooperation.
(Join hands.)

Working
(Step forward.)

Together
(Step back.)

We're all on one team!
(All raise hands.)

Time for a Story!

Craig and Chris, who are twins, are planning their birthday party. But neither one can agree with the other. Will the party be canceled?

Operation — Cooperation

Craig and Chris are twins. They look alike, but they aren't at all the same. Craig likes to plan and organize. Chris would rather let things happen on their own.

Three weeks before their birthday, they decided to get ready for their birthday party. "Let's make a list of everyone we want to invite," suggested Craig.

"I'll just tell my friends about it when I see them," Chris said.

"Then we won't know who can come and who can't," said Craig.

To which Chris replied, "So? What's wrong with that?"

"It just won't work," Craig insisted.

"We can all play games in the backyard," said Chris, changing the subject.

"What games will we play?" asked Craig.

"I don't know. Whatever everybody feels like playing," said Chris.

"But that's no good," said Craig. "We need to plan the games ahead of time."

"No, we don't," said Chris. "What if we plan games that nobody wants to play?"

"If they come to our party, they have to play," Craig said.

"That doesn't sound like much fun to me," Chris answered.

"Well then, forget it! Who needs a stupid party anyway!" Craig stomped off to his room.

Craig sat on his bed with his chin in his hands. Chris went to his room and sat on his bed with his chin in his hands.

Then Chris got up and walked across the hallway to Craig's room. "May I come in?" he said.

"I guess," Craig said, without moving.

"We need a plan," said Chris.

"That's what I've been trying to tell you!" Craig nearly shouted.

"We'll call our plan, 'Operation— Cooperation!'" said Chris.

"I'm glad you're seeing things my way," said Craig. He took a piece of paper and a pencil from his desk drawer. "Now, who shall we invite?"

"Tell you what," said Chris. "You decide who's coming to the party. I'll figure out the games. We have to trust each other to do his job."

"Well, I suppose so," Craig said, but he wasn't quite sure.

When the day of the party came, ten of Craig and Chris's friends showed up. Craig had made sure to invite those people he knew Chris would enjoy.

At game time, Chris led everybody to the backyard. In a big pile were all kinds of balls, bats, hockey sticks, and other games. "Everybody gets to choose a game to play. After ten minutes, we'll switch games. At the end of our play time, everybody will get a prize."

"Great idea!" all the friends agreed.

When the party ended, Craig and Chris said good-bye to their friends. "Thanks for coming to our party!" they said.

"This was the best party ever," they both agreed.

Operation—Cooperation was a great success! ∎

Discussion Questions

1. Are you more like Craig or Chris?

2. Which twin had the better idea? Craig, who wanted to plan everything? or Chris, who wanted to see what happened? (The answer is: Neither way was right or wrong! It's okay to have different styles, as long as you find ways to work together.)

3. What do you think might have happened if Craig and Chris hadn't agreed to cooperate?

4. Is it hard to trust somebody else to do a job their own way?

5. When Craig and Chris decided to cooperate together, what was the result?

1-2-3—ACTIVITIES!

The following activities will help reinforce the value of cooperation. Where appropriate, Activity Sheets can be duplicated for each child.

ACTIVITY 1—"PEACEFUL PUPPET PIECES," p. 18

Supplies needed:

> Activity Sheet 1
> crayons
> scissors
> brads

Activity 1 has children build their own puppet, but there's one catch! Everyone needs to work together or else the puppet won't be complete.

Divide into groups of ten. On Activity Sheet 1 are different puppet pattern pieces. Each person chooses one piece: an arm, a leg, a hand, a foot, a head, a body. Each child can design the piece however he or she chooses (for example, the head can have hair of any style).

Using small brads, each group puts their puppet together. Give the puppet a name, and create a story about how each puppet finds a peaceful way to cooperate with the other puppet people.

> **HOME SCHOOL TIP**
>
> **It takes only two people to do this project, as long as the pieces are divided and everyone participates in building the puppet.**

ACTIVITY 2—"SUGGESTION STEW," p. 19

Supplies needed:

> Activity Sheet 2   one stew pot
> crayons   scissors
> a book (for the role-play)

We often find ourselves in a situation where it takes cooperation with another person in order to find a happy resolution to a problem. Activity 2 encourages children to share their ideas with one another as to how a problem might be resolved using cooperation.

The problem: Benjamin and Brooke both want to read the same book at the same time. How can they cooperate so both will be happy?

Cut out the suggestion strips on Activity Sheet 2 and put them in the stew pot, reading the suggestions aloud as you do so. Then have children write down more suggestions using the blank suggestion strips provided. Each child can put more than one suggestion into the stew pot.

After all the suggestions are in the stew pot, take them out one-by-one and read them aloud. Each suggestion should be applauded. *Discuss:* What are the suggestions that Benjamin and Brooke might try? Are there other suggestions that weren't mentioned?

As an extension activity, act out Benjamin and Brooke's problem in a simple role-play. Two children play the roles of Benjamin and Brooke. They fight over who gets the book first. Have another child reach into the stew pot and pull out a suggested solution. Then have the "actors" try out the suggestion and see what happens.

ACTIVITY 3—"LILY AND LOU NEED YOU!" p. 20

Supplies needed:

Activity Sheet 3

This activity invites children to consider successful and unsuccessful ways of solving problems. The successful ways involve cooperation.

Lily and Lou find themselves in several situations. Each situation is portrayed in a picture and a suggested solution is given. If the solution is one that involves cooperation, have children circle the happy face. If the solution is one that promotes hostility, have them circle the sad face.

Name _____

Peaceful Puppet Pattern Pieces

Cooperation

Suggestion Stew

Problem: Benjamin and Brooke both want to read the same book at the same time. How can they cooperate together so both will be happy?

- They can take turns reading to each other.

- They can flip a coin and call "heads" or "tails" and see who goes first.

- They can find another book they both like and each can read one book, then the other.

Cooperation

Lily and Lou Need You!

Lily and Lou need you! Help Lily and Lou find ways to cooperate with each other.

Look at the first picture and see what the problem is. Then look at the second picture. Does the second picture give a good answer that helps Lily and Lou cooperate? If it does, circle the happy face. If it doesn't, circle the sad face. Can you think of a better way?

1

2

Community Connection

How can your community enhance cooperation? Here are some ideas:

■ **Get involved in a Neighborhood Watch program.**

Many communities have active Neighborhood Watch programs. Such programs enable people to cooperate together to stop crime and vandalism by setting up ways for neighbors to watch out for neighbors. If there is a program in your community, get involved. If there is not, learn more about this organization and get one started.

■ **Speak up for teamwork.**

The competition that is fostered among children and adults through organized sports can easily get out of hand. Work with coaches and team leaders to find ways of making competition less harmful. Teams can join together for an after-game snack; team members can be encouraged to cheer when an opponent makes an outstanding play; team members can build their team spirit by celebrating their own gifts, not by comparing themselves to other teams.

Every effort toward cooperation helps, even if it seems small. If even one team learns the value of cooperation, that's reason to rejoice. Maybe next year, the advances in cooperation can build upon themselves.

■ **Call the local newspaper.**

Talk to the reporters who regularly write about the community news. Suggest a column that highlights ways that people in the community can cooperate with one another. For example, hold fundraisers to help families in need due to fire, flood, illness, and so on. Invite readers to call or write in their suggestions. Share these with your children. The column itself becomes a cooperative effort—it can only happen if everyone cooperates in telling their stories!

Reading List

The Best Baby-Sitter Ever
by Richard Scarry

When Hilda Hippo baby-sits, a little pig discovers that cooperation is much more fun than saying "I won't!"

Dragon Soup
by Arlene Williams

Tonlu helps two Cloud Dragons reach a peaceful solution to their argument about which dragon makes the best soup.

Let's Make a Garden
by Tamara Awad Lobe

Children from around the world join together to create a very special garden.

Old Mahoney and the Bear Family
by Wolfram Hanel

Old Mahoney, a fisherman, and Big Bill, a bear, learn that there's room for everyone when everyone cooperates together.

Stone Soup: An Old Tale
by Marcia Brown

The classic tale of three hungry soldiers and how they entice a village of French peasants to cooperate in making enough soup to feed everybody

The Troubled Village
by Simon Henwood

When the sky falls, the people of a little village must cooperate together to save their homes and lives.

CHAPTER 2

Courage

Before You Begin

Much More Than Being Brave

L. Frank Baum's classic story *The Wizard of Oz* tells about the quest of Dorothy and her companions—a brainless scarecrow, a heartless tin man, and a cowardly lion—to find what they believe that they are missing. At the end of the story, each discovers that home, brain, heart, and courage were part of who they were all along.

The Cowardly Lion learns that courage is more than just being brave. Courage is sticking up for what is right, even in the face of conflict. It is admitting our mistakes and accepting the consequences. Courage is facing a problem or situation and not running away.

But courage also is knowing when to walk away from a situation. Giving Bobby a bloody nose on the playground because he called you a name doesn't solve the problem. Telling Bobby, "I don't like it when you call me that, but I'm not

going to let you bother me," may take more courage than swinging out with a hard punch to the face.

Like every value, we need courage in every aspect of our lives: at home, school, and work. There is no way to avoid difficult situations that require us to take a stand. We cannot close our eyes to injustice and wrongdoing, but having the courage to speak out is not the easiest answer for many people. That's why it is important to teach children what courage means—and what it does not.

Society does not always reward courage. The child who walks away from a fight may be ridiculed. The teenager who refuses to take drugs may be rejected by her peers. The adult who speaks up in a company meeting and goes against the majority vote may find himself without a job. It takes a lot of courage to be courageous!

Yet courage is its own reward. As children recognize the self-esteem that comes from "doing the right thing," and not just going along with the crowd, they will find an inner satisfaction that is far more rewarding than having their behavior governed solely on what other people do and say.

The Cowardly Lion found out that he had more courage than he ever imagined. Our job as adults is to help children discover this same truth, as well as to give them the positive affirmation they need to be courageous, whether that means facing the facts or walking away.

To the Family

Dear Family:

Courage is a complicated value because it is often misunderstood. To many people, courage means fighting back. Yet, sometimes, courage may mean walking away.

Courage is not always rewarded in today's society. That's why it's important for you to help reinforce instances of courage shown by your child.

■ Encourage small acts of courage.

To learn courage, children need to start with small victories. Be sure to encourage and congratulate your child when he or she:

*   Tries a new food
*   Greets a friend or neighbor
*   Refuses to be pushed around by another child

Praise the attempt, not just the end result. The child may try a new food and decide it is awful! Thank the child for at least trying. Never punish a child for failure, if the child has given some effort. This will lead to discouragement and unwillingness to try anything new. Echo the old adage, "If at first you don't succeed, try, try again!" and help your child see failure as a challenge, not a defeat.

■ Admit when you are wrong.

Yes, there are times (plenty of them!) when parents make mistakes. Admitting these mistakes to your child allows the child to do the same. "I'm sorry I yelled at you when you came in the door," Mom said to Sam. "I was having a bad day. It wasn't your fault." The next time Sam gets snappy because he's in a bad mood, he may be able to say, "I'm in a bad mood today, and I'm sorry I slammed my door." You are the best role model your child has—make the most of it!

■ Avoid using shame or fear to force false courage.

Telling a child, "big boys don't cry," only makes him ashamed of his feelings. Let the child express the emotion. Sometimes, tears and fears are masking a deeper issue. Teddy's fear of being alone in bed at night may have something to do with the fact that his best friend Jason's parents are divorcing, and Jason and his sister are each going to live with a different parent.

Forcing a child to "buck up" and not share emotions does not lead to courage. Giving the child tools with which to deal with the emotions allows the courage to develop on its own.

■ Give your child tools to help him or her take control.

It's a terrible feeling for anyone to feel out of control in a situation. Giving children tools to help them cope with situations may, in itself, enhance their courage. For example, Jeff is frightened at the thought of eating dinner at a friend's house. "What if they make me eat something I don't like?" he asks. Saying, "You just eat whatever they give you or you'll never be invited back!" does not give Jeff courage.

Instead, help Jeff think through options. "You can say, 'No, thank you,' when offered an item of food you don't like, or 'I would rather have another helping of mashed potatoes.' Jeff, what are some other things you can say or do that will help you eat dinner at your friend's house without being afraid?"

Consider the consequences of various actions, so the child will feel prepared to handle whatever might come up. And, if the situation comes out on a negative note, work through that as well. "What could you do next time?" or even, "Why don't we have your friend come to our house for dinner?"

It takes courage to learn from our failures, as well as from our successes. If we take the attitude that we are all lifelong learners, we're heading in the right direction.

Let's Get Started!

Are you afraid of the dark? Maybe the plants outside your bedroom are blowing in the wind, and it sounds like fingers tapping. Perhaps the streetlight casts spooky-looking shadows on your walls. Or you're staying overnight at a friend's house, and you hear strange noises that you've never heard before.

We all have times when we are afraid, no matter how old we are. Can you guess what I'm afraid of? (An adult asks the question, and then gives an answer.) We might be afraid of something small, like spiders, or something big, like moving to a new home. No matter what we fear, we should not be ashamed.

Have any of you seen the movie or read the story of *The Wizard of Oz?* One of the characters in the story is the Cowardly Lion, who is even afraid of his own tail. The Cowardly Lion joins the others following the Yellow Brick Road to get to the Emerald City, where they hope to find help. Along the way, they meet all kinds of scary creatures who try to stop them. In the end, the Cowardly Lion finds out he is not the coward he thought he was. He is actually very brave. But that does not mean he is never afraid!

Courage means more than just being brave. While we learn about the value of courage, we'll be finding out all the many ways we can practice courage. Like the Cowardly Lion, you may be surprised to find out how much courage you already have!

Now it's time to learn our fingerplay on courage.

Fingerplay

TO THE TUNE OF
"Frère Jacques" OR *"Where Is Thumbkin?"*

What is courage?

(Shrug shoulders.)

What is courage?

(Shrug shoulders.)

Being brave!

(Raise arms like a bodybuilder.)

Being brave!

(Raise arms like a bodybuilder.)

Saying, "No! I won't fight!"

(Place hands on hips.)

Always doing what's right.

(Put thumbs up.)

Courage counts!

(Raise pointer finger.)

Courage counts!

(Raise pointer finger.)

Time for a Story!

It takes a lot of courage to do what is right, whether that means facing a problem and dealing with it or knowing when to leave it alone. This is the story of a girl named Jasmine and how she used the value of courage even when she was afraid.

Cry Baby

Jasmine loved to ride the bus to school. It gave her time to daydream, or to talk to her friends.

"Cry baby! Cry baby!" Jasmine heard some of the children calling out one day on the bus. She turned around in her seat to see who was crying.

Three rows back, a girl named Tanya sat sobbing, her face in her hands. All around her, the children laughed and pointed. "Tanya is a cry baby!" The bus driver did not see what was going on, and nobody tried to stop the kids from teasing Tanya.

"What happened?" Jasmine asked her friend Angie as they walked home after being dropped off at their bus stop.

"Tanya sat in Al's seat, and when he told her to get out, she started to cry," Angie said. "Then everyone started calling Tanya a cry baby."

Jasmine felt sorry for Tanya, but she was afraid of Al. Al was always picking on somebody or pinching people when nobody else was looking.

The teasing went on for several days. Jasmine felt sick to her stomach and tried to ignore the kids who kept picking on Tanya.

One night, Jasmine could not sleep. She wanted to help Tanya, but she did not know how. If she said something to the bus driver, Al might start picking on her and she knew she'd cry, just like Tanya. But Jasmine could not stand the thought of poor Tanya having to ride the bus every day while Al and his buddies got away with being so mean.

The next day, when Jasmine got on the bus, she saw Tanya sitting by herself. Al sat in back of Tanya, pulling her hair and laughing. When he saw that Jasmine was watching him, Al stuck out his tongue and made a mean face at Jasmine. Jasmine sat down in her seat and quickly looked away.

continued on page 30

Then Jasmine took a deep breath. She got up out of her seat and moved back to where Tanya sat. Tanya pulled away, expecting that Jasmine had come to tease her. Instead, Jasmine said, "Hi, my name is Jasmine. May I sit next to you?"

Tanya smiled, and shook her head yes. Jasmine sat down.

When Al got out of his seat, he walked down the aisle, turned around, and glared at Jasmine and Tanya. Jasmine looked back at Al, right in the eye, even though deep inside she had never been so scared. Al passed by, and sat with his friends.

Every day after that, Jasmine sat with Tanya. Little by little, the other children started talking to Tanya too. Even Al left her alone, now that Tanya had friends.

Soon Jasmine no longer felt afraid of Al. In fact, Jasmine felt quite proud of herself. She realized that she had more courage than she ever knew. ■

Discussion Questions

1. Have you ever been called a mean name? How did that make you feel?

2. Are there other ways that Jasmine could have helped Tanya?

3. Would it have been okay for Tanya to hit Al so he would leave her alone?

4. When you are afraid of something, what do you do? Do you talk to a parent or friend?

5. What do you think Tanya will do the next time someone calls her a name?

1-2-3 Activities!

The following activities will help reinforce the value of courage. Where appropriate, Activity Sheets can be duplicated for each child.

ACTIVITY 1—"FOLLOW THE YELLOW BRICK ROAD TO COURAGE," p. 33

Supplies needed:

> Activity Sheet 1
> crayons or colored pencils
> scissors

Duplicate Activity Sheet 1 for each child. Have children color the bricks yellow and cut them out.

As the lesson on courage develops, encourage children to tell about times when they have been afraid or had to confront a difficult situation. Use their stories to point out examples of courage. After sharing their stories, children can write their names on plain yellow paper bricks and add them to a wall among other plain bricks. Make sure every child gets to have their name on a brick.

Children do not have to "fight back" or hide their feelings to show courage. No child should be ridiculed for being afraid. The idea is to show children that being afraid does not mean that they are cowards. Remember, we are learning courage, and we can do this even when we're not feeling very brave!

ACTIVITY 2—"EVERYONE IS A HERO!" p. 34

Supplies needed:

> Activity Sheet 2
> large roll of paper
> camera (optional)
> crayons or colored pencils

Cut a large sheet of paper from a roll. Along one long edge, write the words, "Everyone Is a Hero!" in bold letters. Take each child's photograph, using an instamatic camera, or ask the children to draw a picture of themselves.

Each child names an example of when they were a hero—how they have shown courage. Some examples might be "rode the school bus by myself," "tried a new food," "raised my hand to answer a question in class," "told the truth when I did something wrong." Use the answers to help illustrate the poster. Children are allowed to "copy" another child's answer. If you have a small group, children may give more than one example.

Everyone in the class, including the teacher, gets to have their picture placed on the "Everyone Is a Hero!" paper.

ACTIVITY 3—"MY COURAGEOUS CRITTER," p. 35

Supplies needed:

> Activity Sheets 3, 4
> colored pencils or crayons
> scissors
> glue or paste

Instead of a Cowardly Lion, each child creates a Courageous Critter. The critter can be a whole animal or a composite of various animals: the head of a cow, the body of a kangaroo, the tail of a monkey. The child names the Courageous Critter and gives the reasons why the critter is courageous (e.g., "My Critter has kangaroo legs so he can hop away from trouble!"). Or, the child can make up a story that tells about the critter.

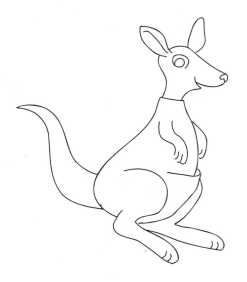

Courage

Follow the Yellow Brick Road to Courage

Courage

Everyone Is a Hero!

I was a hero when I _____

_____

_____

_____

_____

_____

_____

_____ .

Courage

My Courageous Critter

Cut out the animal parts on the next page (or draw your own) and create your own Courageous Critter on a separate sheet of paper. Name your critter and tell why your critter is courageous!

MY COURAGEOUS CRITTER'S NAME IS: _____

MY CRITTER IS COURAGEOUS BECAUSE:

_____

_____

_____

_____

_____

_____

_____

_____

_____

_____

_____

_____

_____

Courage

Courageous Critter Patterns

Community Connection

■ **Discover local heroes.**

Every day, people in your community put their lives on the line in order to do their job. Firefighters, police, and construction workers are just a few of the types of people who show courage every day.

Arrange to visit a local fire station or police headquarters, or call a business that operates construction equipment. Ask if it would be possible to take a tour of the facilities and to learn from the actual people how they practice courage in frightening situations.

■ **Find courage anywhere.**

Ask a medical doctor to talk to the children about his or her career. What led that person into medicine? Can she tell you some situations when she was scared and had to rely on courage to keep her going? Doctors and medical personnel face life-threatening situations all the time. If they let their fear get the best of them, they wouldn't be able to do their work.

Send a letter of appreciation to a doctor or nurse who has helped you when you were sick or in the hospital. We can all appreciate the everyday acts of courage that give life value.

■ **Check the local paper.**

If you don't have time to read the entire newspaper, scan the headlines for instances of courage. The train conductor who climbed to the front of the train to save a baby on the tracks. The father who donated one of his kidneys so his critically ill son could live. There are tremendous acts of courage going on around us all the time.

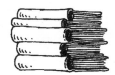

Reading List

Brave Lion, Scared Lion
by Joan Stimson

A shy lion cub, Jasper, saves the day when his brave brother Jake is trapped by crocodiles.

Helen Keller: Courage in the Dark
by Johanna Hurwitz

Helen Keller is known for her courage, but it took the courage of a young teacher named Annie Sullivan to help Helen discover the gifts within herself.

The Legend of the Bluebonnet
by Tomie dePaola

A young girl's courage helps her people in a time of famine.

Minty: A Story of Young Harriet Tubman
by Alan Schroeder

Young Harriet Tubman was a spirited girl who grew up as a slave on a plantation. Her courage and bravery helped many slaves find freedom.

The Empty Pot
by Demi

A group of children are given seeds to grow for the old emperor, not knowing that the seeds won't grow. Ping is the only child with the courage to face the emperor with an empty pot.

Rainbow Fish to the Rescue
by Marcus Pfister

Rainbow Fish is torn between going along with his new group of friends and letting a lonely striped fish who lacks a shiny scale join the group. When a scary shark appears, Rainbow Fish must decide if he should risk losing his friends—and maybe even his life—to save the little striped fish.

CHAPTER 3

Friendship

> *"A friend is someone who knows you as you are,*
> *Understands where you have been*
> *Accepts who you've become,*
> *And still, gently, invites you to grow."*
>
> (Anonymous)

Before You Begin

The Best Gift of All

There is no better gift than the gift of a true friend. If you made a list of all the qualities you seek in a friend, what would they be? Somebody who knows you at your best and at your worst? Somebody with whom you can share your secrets and your dreams? Somebody who sticks by you no matter what? Somebody who really, truly likes who you are? Somebody you can trust? What are the values of friendship you hold most dear?

Everyone has their own idea of what a friend should be like. Instead of making a list of what we consider to be important in a friend, perhaps we should ask a different question: If you had to list the qualities that make you a good friend, what would they be?

We can't force people to be the kind of friend we would choose. But we can choose to be the kind of friend we most cherish.

Children are naturally drawn to other children. Often it seems as though children make friends much more easily than adults. Put a room full of children together, and inevitably, most of them will find somebody with whom they can strike up a friendship. Yet learning what it takes to build a lasting friendship is a skill we develop over time, and with practice.

Where do we begin?

We begin with learning to identify the qualities that are most important to us. Are they sincerity, honesty, humor? How about respect, integrity, loyalty? Be intentional about defining these qualities, and think about friends you've had who have exhibited these traits to you.

An interesting assignment would be for each of us to talk to those people we call our dearest friends. Ask them what it is about your friendship that they value the most. Talk about the good and bad times you've shared and how you've been a friend to one another. Share your hopes about the directions your friendship will take in the next few years. It can be a real eye-opener to find out what your friends value most about your friendship.

As we take time to teach children about friendship, stay alert! Watch the interactions that children have with one another. Observe how they treat one another. Celebrate with them the friendships that give them joy. Learn what you can from the children.

Robert Louis Stevenson once said that "A friend is a present you give yourself." When you give the gift of friendship, you give—and receive—the best gift of all.

To the Family

Dear Family:

What does it mean to be a true friend?

Listed here are some ways that all family members can discover the answer to this question together.

■ **Remember: Parents don't have to be their child's best friend.**

All parents want to be liked by their children. We want to enjoy our children, and we want them to enjoy being with us. There are times, however, when being a parent is more important than being a friend.

Parents are needed to set guidelines and limitations, to correct poor behavior, to help children make good choices. Children don't always agree with the ways parents choose to raise them. It's the job of the parent to enforce the boundaries that protect a child and allow that child to learn and grow within the proper limits.

When a child protests a given bedtime, the parent needs to stay firm. A friend might say, "Sure, stay up as long as you like!" But a parent should say, "I know you want to stay up later, but you have to get up early tomorrow. Maybe on Friday night you can stay up a little longer." The child may not be happy with the decision, but still that child needs the parent to set reasonable limits.

■ **Encourage your child to develop friendships with other adults that you trust.**

As children grow, they need other adults who cherish and care for them. Friendships with other trustworthy adults can help children through difficult times and can also enhance a child's sense of being loved. In a day and age where it is necessary to teach children to be wary of strangers, it is also necessary to help children find adults they can trust, who will listen to them, and who will enjoy being with them.

The adults your child will most likely develop friendships with are those adults who are also a part of your lives. Make sure that you choose responsible and honest friends. Watching your interactions with your friends and being in a home where friendships are treasured helps your child understand the values that are important when choosing a friend.

■ Read books to your child that exemplify a true friend.

There is a reading list for each of the ten values taught in the book *The Value-Able Child: Teaching Values at Home and School*, by Kathleen Long Bostrom (Good Year Books, © 1999). If you do not have a copy of this book, ask your child's teacher for a copy of any reading list you are interested in. Use the reading list for friendship, or go to the library and ask the librarian to help you find books about friendship. Books are a great way to encourage conversation with your child about the true meaning of friendship. Let your child know what you treasure in a friend, and let your child tell you too.

■ Make your home a place where children are welcome.

The best way to get to know the friends your child chooses is to have those children in your home. Invite your child's friends over to play. Create an environment where there is laughter and joy. Don't worry about a few messes. It's worth it to have a home where children feel comfortable bringing their friends. It's also a way to teach your children the ways in which you expect them to behave when they are visiting at their friend's house. "Before I take Carl home, you can both pick up the toys you've played with. Then next time you play at Carl's house, you can help clean up there." Make a game out of it! "I'll set the clock and we'll see how fast you can put those toys away!" What child can resist a good challenge!

■ Celebrate the friendships your child has with other children.

Let your child know the qualities you appreciate in their friends: "I like the way Jesse is polite when he calls you." Children will become defensive if you criticize their friends too harshly, so try the positive approach. Make sure your criticisms are valid. Telling your child that you don't like a friend because she chews with her mouth open may be too picky. But saying to your child, "I'm not happy with the way Cody teases your sister when he plays here. What should we do about that?" allows room for change and discussion, while still letting you hold fast to your values.

Teaching children what it means to be a good friend even when others are not goes a long way in helping your child be guided by the values that are necessary in a healthy society. While you're at it, make sure you take time to build your own friendships! A good friendship takes time and attention, but it is all worth the effort.

Let's Get Started!

Can you imagine a world without friends? It certainly would be a lonely life if there were no such thing as friends!

Friends are some of the most important people in our lives. Along with our families, our friends are the people who love us best. Friends make us smile; friends make us laugh; friends let us cry; friends share our good times and our bad times.

What do you look for in a friend? (Let the children give their answers.) There are many different characteristics that make a friend special to us.

What about you? What makes you a good friend to somebody else? Do you listen when your friend talks? Do you stand up for your friend when someone is being mean? What are the ways that you can be a friend?

Friends come in all shapes and sizes, all colors and styles. Our friends don't have to be exactly like us. In fact, sometimes it's more fun to have a friend who is different. We can learn a lot from our friends!

Our fingerplay will help us remember some of the important qualities of a good friend. Let's get started!

Fingerplay

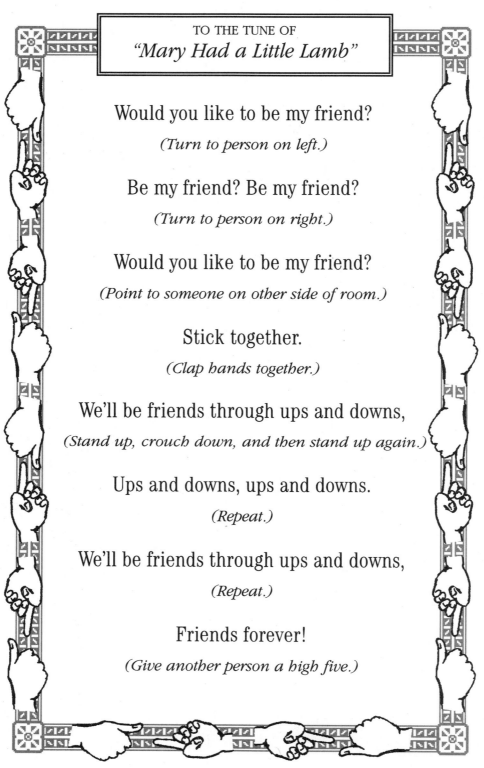

TO THE TUNE OF
"Mary Had a Little Lamb"

Would you like to be my friend?

(Turn to person on left.)

Be my friend? Be my friend?

(Turn to person on right.)

Would you like to be my friend?

(Point to someone on other side of room.)

Stick together.

(Clap hands together.)

We'll be friends through ups and downs,

(Stand up, crouch down, and then stand up again.)

Ups and downs, ups and downs.

(Repeat.)

We'll be friends through ups and downs,

(Repeat.)

Friends forever!

(Give another person a high five.)

Time for a Story!

Wouldn't life be lonely if we didn't have friends? Friends make the world a happy place to live. But sometimes, friends can disappoint each other. Find out what happens when Josie discovers that Courtney isn't quite the friend she thought she was.

Best Friends

Josie and Courtney were the very best of friends. At least, that's what Josie thought.

Whenever Josie's family went to the park, Josie invited Courtney along. They played in the sandbox, hung from the monkey bars, and spun around in circles until they fell to the ground in giggles.

Josie and Courtney planned a sleepover at Josie's house. They made a list of all the games they would play, the movies they would watch, the crafts they would make. "We'll draw pictures for each other," said Josie. And Courtney agreed.

The day before the sleepover, Courtney called Josie. "I can't stay at your house tomorrow night," she said.

"But why not?" asked Josie. "We have everything planned!" Courtney would not tell Josie why she couldn't come to her house. That night, Josie cried herself to sleep.

Josie woke up the next morning, still feeling sad. She took a pad of paper and her crayons and drew pictures by herself.

In the afternoon, Josie called Courtney's house. Courtney's mother answered the phone. "Is Courtney there?" she asked.

"No," said Courtney's mother. "Courtney is spending the night at Kelly's house."

Josie could not believe what she had heard. "But Courtney was supposed to come to my house tonight, and she told me yesterday she couldn't spend the night."

Courtney's mother sounded surprised. "I'm so sorry, Josie. I don't know why Courtney didn't tell me that."

Josie spent the evening watching the movies with her parents. Her mom and dad tried to cheer her up, but nothing seemed to help. She couldn't stop wondering why Courtney didn't want to spend the night.

continued on page 46

The next day, Courtney came over to Josie's house. "Can you play?" she asked. Josie wanted to slam the door in Courtney's face. Instead, she began to cry.

"Why didn't you want to spend the night at my house last night?" she asked Courtney. "I thought you were my friend."

Courtney looked ashamed. "I'm sorry, Josie. It's just that I've been wanting to be friends with Kelly for such a long time, and when she invited me to spend the night, I didn't want to say no. I thought you'd understand."

"Well, I don't understand," Josie said. "Friends don't do that kind of thing to each other."

"I'm sorry," Courtney answered. "You're right. I should have told Kelly no. Or I should have told you what had happened. I haven't been a very good friend to you."

Josie wiped the tears from her face. "You can come in and play if you want to."

Courtney hugged Josie. "You are such a great friend!" she said. "I won't do anything like that again. Besides, I didn't have a very good time. Kelly wouldn't even share any of her toys with me."

Josie led Courtney into the living room. "Here you go," she said, handing Courtney a stack of drawings. "I made these for you."

Courtney smiled. "Thanks, Josie."

"You're welcome," Josie said.

"Can we still be friends?" Courtney asked.

"Let's just forget what happened and start all over again," Josie said.

"And the next time Kelly calls and asks me to play, I'll tell her, 'I can't today. I'm playing with my best friend!'"

"Let's go play," Josie answered. And the two girls scampered off to Josie's room, friends again. ■

Discussion Questions

1. How would you feel if your best friend acted like Courtney?

2. If Courtney wanted to play with Kelly, what could she have said to Josie?

3. Did Josie do the right thing by keeping her friendship with Courtney?

4. What should Josie do when she gets invited to Courtney's house?

5. Can you think of a different way the story might have ended?

1-2-3 Activities!

The following activities will help reinforce the value of friendship. Where appropriate, Activity Sheets can be duplicated for each child.

ACTIVITY 1—"PLANTING SEEDS OF FRIENDSHIP," p. 49

Supplies needed:

> Activity Sheet 1
> crayons or colored pencils
> scissors

A good friendship grows like a plant. First, a seed is planted. When the seed sprouts, it needs to be fed, watered, and cared for. For a friendship to grow, it needs kindness, honesty, respect, forgiveness, compassion—many of the values in this book. Activity Sheet 1 helps reinforce many components of a good friendship.

Each child cuts out the petals of the flower. On each petal is one trait of friendship. The petals can be colored with crayons or colored pencils. The petals are pasted on a separate sheet of paper as the child creates a beautiful flower of friendship.

Some of the petals are blank, so that the child can come up with answers too. The completed flower might look like this:

ACTIVITY 2— "THE PERFECT FRIEND," p. 50–51

Supplies needed:

> Activity Sheets 2 and 3
> crayons or colored pencils
> scissors
> paste or glue

Each child will create a "perfect friend" using Activity Sheets 2 and 3. On Activity Sheet 3 is the outline of a body. On Activity Sheet 2 there are different body parts with labels to cut out and paste to the outline: a kind heart, helping hands, understanding eyes, listening ears, a welcoming smile, and a funny bone. The child then completes the picture by drawing additional parts. When the pictures are finished, share with one another: What do you look for in a friend? Are there other parts that should be added to the "perfect friend"?

ACTIVITY 3—"SECRET FRIENDS," p. 52

Supplies needed:

> Activity Sheet 4
> envelopes
> pencils
> crayons

It's fun to have a secret friend—and to be one too! Have each child write his or her name on an envelope. Collect the envelopes. Then pass them back, one to each child, making sure that nobody receives their own name. Do not identify the identity of the secret friends!

HOME SCHOOL TIP

Your child can be a secret friend to a neighbor, friend, or relative. The "secret friend" letter can be mailed to someone outside of the home.

On Activity Sheet 4, the children will draw a picture or write a letter to their secret friend. The Activity Sheets are then folded and placed in an envelope with the name of the secret friend. Collect all the letters and give them out sometime during the study of this chapter on friendship.

The children are to be extra nice to their secret friend. Perhaps at the end of the chapter, the secret friends can be revealed. Or you may choose to keep their identities a secret!

The Value-Able Child, Copyright © 1999 Good Year Books.

Friendship

Planting Seeds of Friendship

A good friendship is like a plant. First, a seed is planted. When the seed sprouts, it needs to be fed, watered, and cared for. But the food and water it takes to grow a friendship are not the same as the food and water a plant needs.

For a friendship to grow, it needs kindness, honesty, respect, forgiveness, compassion. Do you recognize these as values too?

Plant a seed of friendship. Watch the flower grow!

MY FRIENDSHIP FLOWER

Kind

Funny

Caring

Thoughtful

Loyal

_____

_____

_____

Friendship

Name _____

The Perfect Friend

Can you create a perfect friend? Cut out the body parts and labels and paste them in the correct places on the body outline. Then color in your friend.

What do you look for in a friend?

kind heart

helping hands

listening ears

welcoming smile

understanding eyes

funny bone

ACTIVITY SHEET 2

The Value-Able Child, Copyright © 1999 Good Year Books.

Friendship

The Perfect Friend

Friendship

Secret Friends

Dear _____ ,

Surprise! I am your secret friend. I promise to be extra nice to you, even though you don't know who I am. I made you this picture to let you know that I am thinking about you. I hope you enjoy it!

With best wishes from your Secret Friend!

Community Connections

■ **Be a friend to others.**

The best way to make a friend is to be a friend. Invite your neighbors over for a picnic. Get to know an older adult who has no family nearby, and the next time you go to a movie or shopping, invite that person along. Even with people you don't know, treat them like you would a good friend.

■ **Use your smile today.**

As you go throughout your day, make an extra effort to smile at the people that you meet. You may really brighten someone's day by this simple act of friendliness. And you just might make a new friend while you're at it!

■ **Be a secret friend.**

If you've ever received a nice card in the mail signed "Your Secret Pal," you know how nice it is to know that somebody cares about you. Choose someone in the community that you know, perhaps somebody who is going through a difficult time, or someone who is especially kind to others. Every month, find a reason to send a card, and sign it "From Your Secret Friend."

It may be possible to talk to the supervisor of the local hospital and ask if you can bring a flower to somebody who is alone or struggling with a long-term illness. You can be a secret friend, or you can let the person know who you are. A little expression of friendship can go a long way.

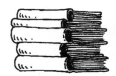

Reading List

Frederick
by Leo Lionni

Frederick, a mouse who loves daydreaming and poetry, helps his friends through a dreary, cold winter.

New Friends, True Friends, Stuck-Like-Glue Friends
by Virginia Kroll

Cheerful lyrics present the many different sides of friendship.

The Woman Who Named Things
by Cynthia Rylant

A lonely, old woman discovers a new friend.

Poppleton and Friends
by Cynthia Rylant

Poppleton the pig shares a delightful day with two good friends.

Friends
by H. Heine

A story about friends who share everything.

The Adventures of Sugar and Junior
by Angela Shelf Medearis

An African American girl, Sugar, makes friends with her next-door neighbor, a Latino boy with the nickname "Junior."

Ada's Pal
by George Ella Lyon

Friendship blossoms between a little girl and her family's two dogs.

55 Friends
by Abbie Zabar

A cumulative rhyming text builds up as fifty-five friends are introduced.

CHAPTER 4

Honesty

Before You Begin

The Best Policy

"I promise to tell the truth, the whole truth, and nothing but the truth." This is the vow a witness takes in a court of law. Yet even if we are never called to testify in a courtroom, it is a good promise by which to live and one that is more difficult to follow than we care to admit. Sometimes, we are inclined to tell the truth, but not the whole truth, and that can be a subtle form of dishonesty in itself.

Every day we are faced with situations that test our honesty. Mr. Jacobs takes his toddler shopping at the grocery store. When they return home, he discovers that the child has tucked a small bag of candy in his pocket. Mr. Jacobs does not feel like driving all the way back to the store to return the candy. Nobody will ever know, and besides, the candy only cost a small amount.

Or Mom tells the kids, "If Mrs. Randall calls, tell her I'm not home," even though she will be home and just doesn't want to talk to Mrs. Randall. What does such a request teach the children about telling the truth? It seems harmless, but in fact, Mom has asked her children to lie.

Then there is the issue of what we refer to as "white lies." A friend comes to work with a new hairstyle and asks you how you like it. You think the new style looks terrible. Do you say this

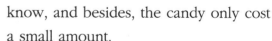
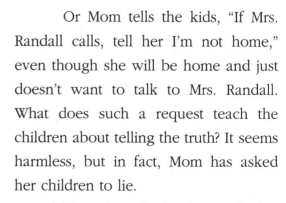

to your friend? Or do you tell a "white lie" so as not to hurt her feelings? How can you be honest without compromising the value of honesty?

Honesty is more than just refusing to tell lies. Honesty is speaking up for what is right, even when it puts the speaker at some risk.

As we approach this chapter on honesty, keep in mind the courtroom vow. Through the use of the stories and activities on honesty, children will discover that honesty definitely is the best policy.

To the Family

Dear Family:

Honesty is one of the keys to successful relationships, trust, and the building of a society where honor is still treasured as one of the cornerstones of healthy families and communities. You can assist your child in learning the value of honesty by the way in which you live.

■ **Be careful what you model.**

Getting in the habit of telling "white lies" sets an example of dishonesty. If you are out with one child and you buy her a new toy, don't tell her, "Now, keep this a secret from your little brother so he won't get mad." Instead, tell your children, "Today I bought a new toy for Susie. When I take Randy shopping next week, I will let him choose something new too."

■ **Remember to affirm your child for telling the truth.**

Henry accidentally broke a water glass. When he told his mother what had happened, she scolded him and sent him to his room. The next time Henry broke something, he did not want to tell his mother what had happened.

Validate your child's honesty: "Henry, you should not have been using that glass. But thank you for telling me what happened. Now, please bring me a broom so I can clean up the broken glass." The next time an accident happens, Henry will be more likely to tell his mother the truth.

■ **Find real-life examples of honesty and dishonesty and discuss the consequences.**

Look through magazines and newspapers, or talk with neighbors or classmates. Find examples where being honest or dishonest resulted in positive or negative consequences. You may even find examples where somebody has been dishonest and not had to suffer any negative consequences. Ask your child, "Is this right?" As much as possible, don't give your child the right answer. Ask questions that allow the child to discover the answer. For example, if your child is playing with another child in the neighborhood and that child tells her mother a lie and isn't caught, ask your child, "What is the best thing to do, even if you've already told a lie?"

■ **Create a story with your child.**

Let the "hero" be the one who is honest. An example:

WHO IS THE HERO?

Don and Charlie were playing ball in their yard. When Charlie accidentally threw the ball over the fence into Mr. Hoffman's yard, Don started to climb the fence to retrieve the ball.

"Wait," Charlie said. "We aren't allowed to go into Mr. Hoffman's yard without asking. Let's go knock on his door and see if he will get the ball for us."

Who is the hero? CHARLIE!

As you and your child share stories and examples about honesty and live this value in your own lives, you'll find that everybody's self-esteem will benefit. Enjoy!

Let's Get Started!

What do you think of when you hear the word *honesty?* Let's write these ideas on the chalkboard (or chart paper). Now, let's think of some words that mean the opposite of *honesty* and write these down next to the other list.

Honesty means telling the truth. It means telling the whole truth. Is it enough to say, "Dad, Teddy broke the window with the baseball," when Teddy did break the window, but only because you didn't catch the ball when Teddy threw it to you? Sometimes we tell lies because we don't want to hurt someone's feelings. For instance, your best friend is wearing a pair of shoes that you don't like. She asks you, "Aren't my new shoes pretty?" Even though you think the shoes are ugly, you don't want your friend to feel bad, so you say, "Yes, I love those shoes!" You don't want to tell her, "Those are the ugliest shoes I've ever seen!" What could you say that would be honest, but not hurt her feelings? (For example: "I'll bet you can run really fast in those shoes!")

Together, we are learning what it means to be honest and to tell the whole truth. Let me know the ways in which you are honest in what you say and do. And if you're having trouble trying to figure out how to be honest and tell the whole truth about something, come to me and talk to me about your problem. Together, we'll work it out.

Let's practice our fingerplay about honesty.

Fingerplay

TO THE TUNE OF
"Rockabye, Baby"

Honesty is the right point of view.

(Point to eyes.)

Always be honest, say what is true.

(Hold up right hand with palm facing out.)

Telling a lie is not right to do,

(Wag fingers back and forth.)

So I'll tell the truth, and hope
you will too.

(Point finger at self, then at others.)

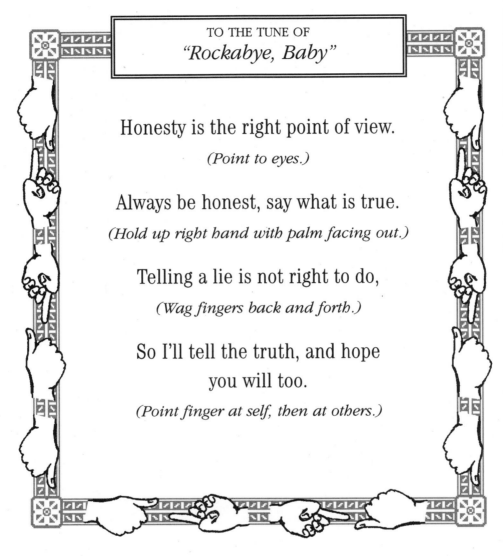

Time for a Story!

This is a story about telling the whole truth. Listen carefully as I read it to you. After I'm finished reading, I need you to help me answer some questions about what it means to tell the whole truth.

Jenny and the Chocolate-Chip Cookies

Mother set a plate of fresh-baked, chocolate-chip cookies on the table. *"Mmmm,"* Jenny sighed, as she walked through the kitchen. "Those cookies smell wonderful! Can I have some?"

"I baked these cookies for the bake sale," Mother answered. "Please don't eat them. I'll bake some cookies for the rest of us tomorrow."

Jenny felt disappointed, but followed her mother's instructions. She went to her room to read, trying not to think about the delicious cookies sitting on the plate in the kitchen.

Knock, knock, knock! Jenny's older brother, Paul, peeked into her room. "Hey, Jenny," he said. "Look what I found in the kitchen. Chocolate-chip cookies! Here, I brought you a couple."

Jenny knew that she shouldn't eat the cookies, but when Paul handed her the cookies, she could not resist.

A little while later, Mother came into Jenny's room. "Jenny," she said. "Some of the cookies I baked for the bake sale are missing. Did you take the cookies from the plate?"

Jenny thought. She *had* eaten the cookies, but she *had not* taken them from the plate.

"No, Mother," Jenny answered. "I did not take the cookies from the plate."

"But I made two dozen cookies, twenty-four, and there are only nineteen left," mother said, sounding frustrated.

Jenny turned around without another word and left the kitchen, returning to her room. She quietly opened her dresser drawer and looked at the cookie she was saving for later. She started to feel very guilty.

Not only had she taken cookies she was told not to take, but she hadn't told her brother the cookies were off-limits, and she hadn't told her mother who ate the cookies. Suddenly Jenny's stomach started to hurt, and she didn't want the cookie in her dresser drawer anymore. ■

Discussion Questions

1. Was Jenny being honest? Did she really tell the truth? Why or why not?

2. Should Jenny have told Paul what Mother said about not eating the cookies?

3. If you were in Jenny's situation, what would you do?

4. What do you think will happen if Jenny goes to her mother and tells her the truth?

5. The next time something like this happens, what should Jenny do?

1-2-3 Activities!

The following activities will help reinforce the value of honesty. Where appropriate, Activity Sheets can be duplicated for each child.

ACTIVITY 1—"WHAT SHOULD YOU DO?" p. 66

Supplies needed:

> Activity Sheet 1
> pencils

Three different situations involving honesty are summed up in brief sentences on Activity Sheet 1. Each situation ends with a question. Following the question are two pictures giving different responses to the question, "What should the person do?" The child circles the answer that best represents the value of honesty.

After the children are finished circling their answers, read through each scenario, one by one. Ask questions such as: "What if Sammy hides the toy and his sister finds out what he did?" "If Jessie keeps Bobby's dollar, will that help her feel good about herself?" "Is it okay for Sherry to tell Rhonda she doesn't want to play with her, even if that might hurt Rhonda's feelings?"

ACTIVITY 2—"A SACK OF LIES," p. 67

Supplies needed:

> Activity Sheet 2
>
> paper grocery sacks, enough for each
>   child on Team One
>
> rocks or blocks or heavy objects,
>   seven for each child on Team Two

"A Sack of Lies" is a role-play game that can involve all the children, or it can be played with only two children who act out the story for the entire class.

Before the story:

Divide the children into two teams. Each team stands in a line. The children in Team One stand side by side with the children in Team Two.

Each child in Team One gets a paper grocery sack. Each child in Team Two gets a stack of seven rocks (or blocks or some other heavy object).

Read the story out loud. Whenever Jodie tells a lie, the children in Group Two place a rock in the bag of their partner from Group One. After each rock is placed in the sack, the child in Group One picks up the sack to see how heavy it is, then sets it back down.

After the story:

Discuss that when Jodie told the first lie, she started a problem that just got worse and worse. By telling one lie, she felt as though she had to keep telling more lies to try and cover up the first lie. By the time the story ended, Jodie had told four lies, and even had asked her best friend to tell a lie too.

The sack of rocks got heavier and heavier each time Jodie told a lie. Sometimes, one lie leads to another until the weight of our lies is so heavy, it makes it difficult to tell the truth.

> **HOME SCHOOL TIP**
>
> You don't need groups to play this game, as long as you have two people. You might choose to take turns being the person with the sack and the person with the rocks.

Discussion Questions

1. What should Jodie have said to Penny when Penny first called?

2. How could Jodie have told the truth and not a lie?

3. Once Jodie told a lie, could she have told Penny the truth before she felt as though she needed to tell more lies?

4. Is it okay to tell a lie if you know you won't get caught?

ACTIVITY 3 —"A PATHWAY TO HONESTY," p. 68

Supplies needed:

> Activity Sheet 3
> pencils

David wants to play with his friend Kyle. But first David's mother has given him a list of chores to do. In order for David to find his way to Kyle's house, he must travel the "Pathway to Honesty" on Activity Sheet 3. The road is filled with many detours and roadblocks that relate to honesty.

Each child traces a path for David through the maze. There are questions along the way that are entitled "roadblocks." When the child reaches a roadblock, a decision needs to be made about how to answer. If the answer is an honest one, the child moves forward on the path. If the answer is dishonest, the child must go back to start. Some questions provide "detours," or situations that set the child back a few spaces but not all the way back to start.

After the children have traced their way through the "Pathway to Honesty," the following questions can be discussed.

Questions

1. Why is it tempting to take the shortcuts?

2. If you aren't honest at the beginning, is there still a chance to go back and do things right?

3. Think of a situation when you were tempted to do something that was not totally honest. How did it make you feel about yourself?

Name _____

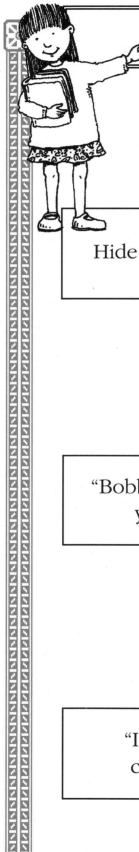

What Should You Do?

1. Sammy broke his sister's new toy.
   What should Sammy do?

| Hide the broken toy. | "I'm sorry I broke your new toy." |

2. Jessie sees a dollar bill fall from Bobby's pocket. She picks it up. What should Jessie do?

| "Bobby, you dropped your dollar." | Keep the dollar for herself. |

3. Rhonda calls Sherry to see if she can play. Sherry does not want to play with Rhonda. What should Sherry do?

| "I am sick and cannot play." | "I don't feel like playing right now." |

ACTIVITY SHEET 1

Name _____

A Sack of Lies

Jodie and Alexa planned to play together after school. When Jodie got home, the phone rang. It was another friend, Penny. Penny asked if Jodie could play.

"No," said Jodie. "I have to clean my room." *(Place a rock in the sack.)*

Alexa called Jodie. "Can you play now?"

"Sure," said Jodie. "I'll be right over."

Jodie started walking to Alexa's house. On the way, she ran into Penny.

"Where are you going?" Penny asked Jodie.

"Oh, just for a walk around the block," Jodie answered. *(Place a rock in the sack.)*

"I thought you had to clean your room," Penny said.

"I do," said Jodie. "As soon as I get back from my walk." *(Place a rock in the sack.)*

Then Penny said, "I'm on my way to Alexa's house. She said I could come over and play with her. She said you were coming over too."

Jodie didn't know what to say. "No, I'm not," she said. *(Place a rock in the sack.)*

Jodie ran home. She called Alexa on the phone. "Please tell Penny that you did not invite me to your house. I will stay home until she leaves. Call me then and I will come over."

(Place three more rocks in the sack, because Jodie asked her friend to lie.)

Discussion: See "After the story," on page 64.

Honesty

A Pathway to Honesty

David wants to play with his friend Kyle. But first, David's mother has given him a list of chores to do. In order for David to find his way to Kyle's house, he must travel the "Pathway to Honesty." The road is filled with many detours and roadblocks. Can you help David find his way?

CHORES:
1. Empty his trash can.
2. Walk the dog.
3. Finish his homework.

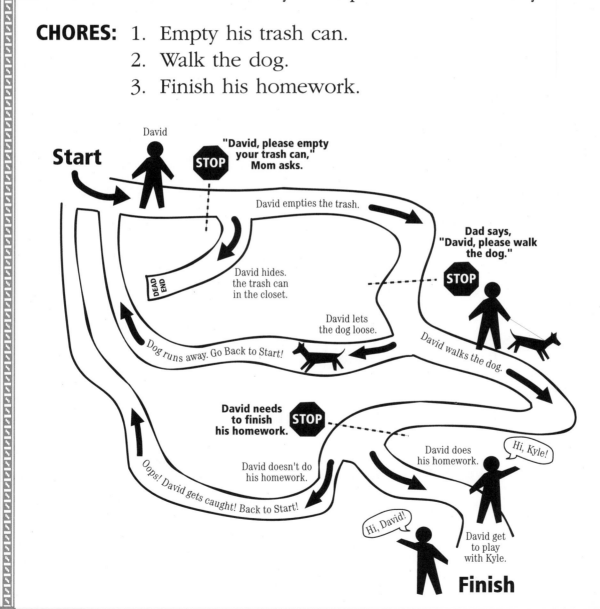

ACTIVITY SHEET 3

Community Connections

■ **Check your local newspaper.**

Find stories in the newspaper about people who have done something honest (e.g., someone finds some money, but instead of keeping it, turns it over to the police). Check with the local library or community center to see if your children can make a bulletin board on which to post all the stories. The title of the bulletin board can be, "Honesty Is the Best Policy!"

■ **Sponsor an "Honesty Hour."**

Hold an "Honesty Hour" during a Scout group or at any other organization where parents and children meet together.

1. Make up a skit about being honest.

2. Find storybooks to read about honesty (see Reading List on p. 71).

3. Play the "Honesty Hot Potato Game."

    •   Before the game begins, each parent and child pair thinks up a situation where someone has the choice to be honest or tell a lie. Write the situation down on a piece of paper and put it in a large box.

    •   Everyone in the group then gathers in a circle. One person has a large potato. The potato is passed around the circle while music is being played.

    •   When the music stops, the person with the potato pulls one of the papers out of the box and reads it aloud. The parent and child together decide on an answer and share it with the group. Then play continues.

Examples of Situations

1. Cindy and Steve are best friends. Cindy sees Steve steal a pencil from the teacher's pencil holder. The teacher asks the class, "Who took my new pencil?" Cindy can:

    a.   Tell Steve to return the pencil.

    b.   Pretend she doesn't know who took the pencil.

2. Maria needs to pick up her dirty clothes before she invites a friend over. Maria can:

   a.   Shove all her dirty clothes under the bed to make her room look clean.

   b.   Put her dirty clothes in the laundry and next time, not leave them on the floor!

3. There is one slice of cake left. Oliver knows that his sister has not had her slice. Oliver can:

   a.   Eat the cake and say that he forgot it was for his sister.

   b.   Ask his sister if he can have a bite.

4. Dad asks Ben to put a letter in the mailbox. Ben sets the letter down on his desk while he finishes a book he is reading. Several days later, Ben finds the letter, still on his desk. Ben can:

   a.   Put the letter in the mailbox when nobody is looking.

   b.   Tell his dad what happened and then mail the letter.

5. Natasha doesn't want to take a bath. She'd rather finish coloring the picture she is drawing. Natasha can:

   a.   Get her hair wet in the sink so it looks like she took a bath and keep on coloring.

   b.   Ask, "Can I finish coloring the picture first and then take my bath?"

Reading List

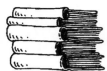

Franklin Fibs
by Paulette Bourgeois

A young turtle tells lies about himself and then is asked to prove them.

A Day's Work
by Eve Bunting

Francisco, a Mexican American boy, tries to help his grandfather find a job in California. When the boy tells lies about his grandfather's ability, trouble results. In the end, honesty helps save the day.

Ira Sleeps Over
by Bernard Waber

Ira worries about spending the night at a friend's house without his beloved teddy bear. Is honesty really the best policy?

Sam, Bangs, and Moonshine
by Evaline Ness

Samantha, a fisherman's daughter, learns the difference between fantasy and truth.

Tales of Peter Rabbit
by Beatrix Potter

A mischievous rabbit gets into trouble with his dishonesty.

Too Many Tamales
by Gary Soto

Maria takes her mother's diamond ring, which she then loses in the dough she's making for the holiday tamales. Maria's reluctance to tell the truth about what she's done leads to a lot of upset stomachs as Maria and her cousins eat all the tamales in search of the ring.

CHAPTER 5

Kindness

Before You Begin

Intentional, Not Random

About two months into the school year, a new boy entered Mrs. Robinson's second-grade class. Howie was bright and advanced academically, but sorely lacking in social skills. He did not know how to interact with the other children and responded in silly and irritating ways when the other children approached him. Soon, the children began to avoid Howie and ridiculed him for his behavior.

In an effort to help integrate Howie into the class, Mrs. Robinson arranged the seating so that Howie would be near three children who were especially good at showing kindness to other students. Mrs. Robinson hoped that the other children would learn to be kind to Howie by observing the actions of the three students seated with him.

One of these students was a girl named Julie. Mrs. Robinson knew that Julie was popular with the other students and that she also had a deep sense of right and wrong. She treated the other students with equal kindness.

Mrs. Robinson worried when Valentine's Day came around. What if the other children refused to give Howie a valentine? Mrs. Robinson emphasized that each child was to bring a valentine for every other child in the class.

On Valentine's Day, Mrs. Robinson distributed the valentines while the children played at recess. As she went through each bag, she noticed that Julie had carefully written her name on the back of each valentine. Then she noticed that one of the valentines from Julie had a message written on it: "I think you are a special person." The valentine was addressed to Howie.

Slowly, and with time, the other children began to reach out to Howie. They included him in their games. Although he still had trouble getting along with some of the children, many of them began to treat him with more kindness. They ignored his poor behavior, yet were quick to compliment him when he did something right. Howie's attention-demanding behavior began to lessen. The powerful example of the kindness of a few children set the tone for the beginning of Howie's acceptance.

Much is made these days of the power of sporadic acts of kindness. Popular newspaper advice columnists encourage readers to send letters giving examples of an act of kindness that they have received at the hands of a friend or stranger. Even basic good manners such as saying "please" and "thank you" can go a long way toward spreading kindness.

In this chapter on kindness, we will explore the ways children can be encouraged to *think* kind thoughts, to *act* out of kindness, and to *engage* in intentional deeds of kindness.

To the Family

Dear Family:

Please be a partner with your child as we learn about the importance of kindness. You can help by doing the following:

■ **Be a model of kindness.**

The tone of voice you use, the way you handle your child's anger, the time you give to listen—all these are important. Your child will look to you to learn what it means to be kind.

■ **Point out incidents of kindness.**

If you hear a story on the news, see someone engaged in an act of kindness, or catch your child being kind, no matter how small the example, be sure to make a point of recognizing the kindness. For example, when your child comforts a baby brother or sister who is crying, tell your child, "Good for you! That was so kind of you to comfort Jack." Affirm any and all acts of kindness on the part of your child and others.

■ **Find ways to show kindness.**

Is there a neighbor who has lost his wife? a family member who is lonely? Find ways that you and your child can be kind to someone in need. A simple phone call, a card that says "Thinking of you," a plate of cookies shared with a neighbor—these are all things in which children can play an active role.

Remember, the more we all model kindness with one another, the more likely it is that kindness will become a good habit that builds on itself.

Let's Get Started!

What does it mean to be kind? Is it how you act or the words that you use?

Both! Kindness is being thoughtful to family, friends, and acquaintances, as well as to people who provide services, such as cashiers, waiters, flight attendants, police officers, and so on. Kindness is using words that do not hurt people's feelings. Kindness is being sensitive to what other people are thinking and feeling.

Can you think of some other words that mean kindness (e.g., *gentleness, thoughtfulness, consideration, friendliness,* and so on)? Let's write these on the chalkboard (or chart paper).

As we learn about kindness, we will practice being kind to other children, to our families, and to people we meet in our communities. You may find out that when you act with kindness, other people are likely to respond with kindness to you too.

We will begin with a fingerplay about kindness.

Fingerplay

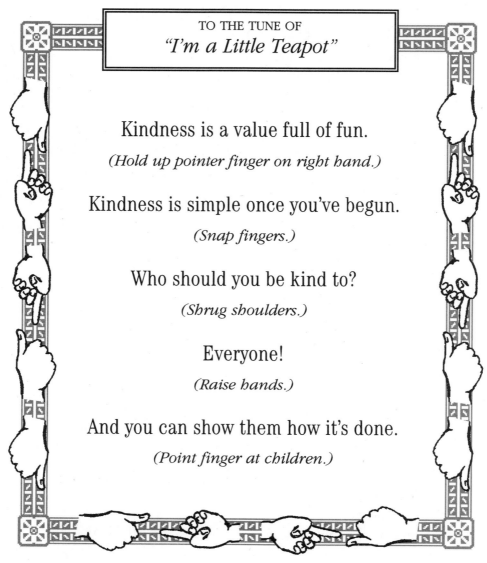

TO THE TUNE OF
"I'm a Little Teapot"

Kindness is a value full of fun.
(Hold up pointer finger on right hand.)

Kindness is simple once you've begun.
(Snap fingers.)

Who should you be kind to?
(Shrug shoulders.)

Everyone!
(Raise hands.)

And you can show them how it's done.
(Point finger at children.)

Time for a Story!

Being the new kid can be frightening and lonely. It may seem as though everyone else in the world has a friend, and nobody needs a new one. But we all need friends! Listen to the story of how a new kid becomes a new friend, just from a simple act of kindness.

The New Kid

Mrs. Goforth began class one day with a special message. "Boys and girls, we have a new student with us today. Jerry and his family have just moved to the area, and Jerry is going to be in our class. Can we show him what a wonderful group we are?"

Jerry sat shyly in his seat. He smiled and blushed. He also looked frightened. Jerry did not know a single person in the room.

At recess, the children gathered with their friends to play. Mary Beth and Alissha got out the jump ropes. John and Stephanie organized a dodge-ball game. The other children climbed the jungle gym, ran races, and built castles in the sandbox. But Jerry stood all alone on the playground.

Mary Beth and Alissha were so busy jumping rope they didn't even notice Jerry. John and Stephanie saw him, but their dodge-ball game was already in progress. Several other children saw Jerry by himself, but they, too, were busy with their own games.

Then Stephanie turned to John. "Why don't we start all over and invite Jerry to play with us?"

"I don't know," said John. "What if the other kids don't want him to play with us? What if they get mad at us?"

"But he looks so lonely," Stephanie said.

The dodge-ball game ended, and it was time to choose sides for a new game. Stephanie and John were team captains. They whispered to one another. They walked over to Jerry.

The other children watched to see what would happen.

"Jerry, would you like to be on my team?" Stephanie asked.

continued on page 78

Jerry looked shyly at the ground.

John spoke up. "Then Jerry gets to be on my team next!" he said.

Jerry looked over at Stephanie and John.

"What do you say, Jerry?" Stephanie asked. "How does that sound?"

"Fine," Jerry said, and smiled.

When recess ended and the children returned to their classroom, Mrs. Goforth watched proudly. Jerry was surrounded by children, and all of them were eager to talk with him.

"You should have seen Jerry at recess!" John said to Mrs. Goforth. "He was the star player."

"I'm not surprised," said Mrs. Goforth. "You are all stars at showing kindness." ■

Discussion Questions

1. Have you ever been the "new kid"? How did it feel?

2. Do you think the other children were being mean when they ignored Jerry?

3. How did Susan and John teach the other children about kindness?

4. Can you share a time when you showed kindness to someone?

5. Think of a way you can show kindness to someone today. How does that make you feel?

1-2-3 Activities!

The following activities will help reinforce the value of kindness. Where appropriate, Activity Sheets can be duplicated for each child.

ACTIVITY 1—"WORD PUZZLES," p. 81

Supplies needed:

Activity Sheet 1
pencils

Activity Sheet 1 includes two word puzzles. Both puzzles can be used, or the second one can be used for younger children.

The first puzzle lists a number of words that are synonyms for *kindness*. The words are hidden in the puzzle. As the words are found, they should be circled in the puzzle and crossed off the list.

The second puzzle asks the child to color in the Xs. The message left will be: "Be Kind to Others."

ACTIVITY 2—"X's AND O's," p. 82

Supplies needed:

Activity Sheet 2
pencils

Activity Sheet 2 consists of a series of pictures. Some of the pictures show examples of a child being kind, and some show examples of being unkind. Each child circles the pictures showing kindness and draws an X through the pictures where someone is being unkind.

The Value-Able Child, Copyright © 1999 Good Year Books.

ACTIVITY SHEET 3—"FILL IN THE PICTURE," p. 83

Supplies needed:

Activity Sheet 3
crayons or colored pencils

Activity Sheet 3 tells a story of how a child can be kind to a new friend. The child draws pictures to illustrate the story. Afterwards, the children can discuss other ways of showing kindness.

Kindness

Name _____

Word Puzzles

I	L	O	V	E	P	C	D
T	R	L	G	O	O	D	P
H	G	E	N	T	L	E	L
A	S	P	K	U	I	W	E
N	T	R	I	M	T	V	A
K	I	N	D	N	E	S	S
Y	B	I	M	P	O	D	E
O	L	C	O	X	Q	N	H
U	H	E	L	P	F	U	L

Find and circle these words:

KINDNESS	HELPFUL	NICE
POLITE	GOOD	LOVE
PLEASE	GENTLE	THANK YOU

(Alternate puzzle)

Color in the X's and find a hidden message!

X	X	B	E	X	X	K	I	N	D	X
T	O	X	X	O	T	H	E	R	S	X

The Value-Able Child, Copyright © 1999 Good Year Books.

ACTIVITY SHEET 1 *Chapter 5:* KINDNESS 81

Kindness

X's and O's

How can you be kind to others?

Draw an O around the pictures that show someone being kind.

Draw an X through the pictures that show someone who is not being kind.

Kindness

Fill in the Picture

I CAN BE KIND TO OTHERS

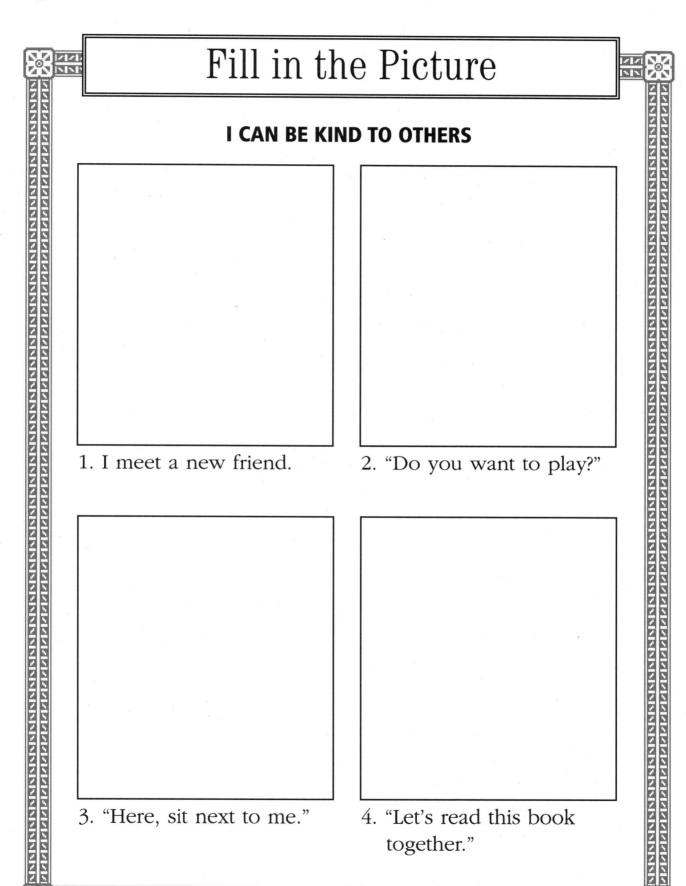

1. I meet a new friend.

2. "Do you want to play?"

3. "Here, sit next to me."

4. "Let's read this book together."

Community Connections

■ **Write a thank-you note.**

Write a thank-you note to someone who has done something nice for you: a librarian, a teacher, a Scout leader. Or write to someone you've never met but who works for the community: the mail carrier, the garbage collector, the mayor, a clerk at the store.

■ **Bake cookies for a new neighbor.**

Watch for moving vans in the neighborhood. Bake a loaf of bread, a batch of cookies, a pie, or a cake, and take it to the new neighbors. Offer to help them find their way around—to the grocery stores, library, parks, and so on.

■ **Contact the local nursing homes or older adult communities to plan a visit.**

Draw a picture to give to a resident at a retirement or nursing home. Many times, older adults in these facilities do not have family nearby and relish the chance to visit with a child. Remember, some of these places get bombarded during the holidays with offers to help. Plan to visit or bring pictures at other times of the year as well.

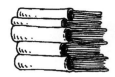

Reading List

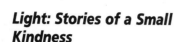

Light: Stories of a Small Kindness
by Nancy White Carlstrom

A collection of short stories based on the theme of kindness

Lucy's Picture
by Nicola Moon

Lucy tries to figure out the best kind of picture she can make for her grandfather, who is blind.

Now One Foot, Now the Other
by Tomie dePaola

A little boy teaches his grandfather how to walk again following a stroke.

The Wednesday Surprise
by Eve Bunting

A young girl and her grandmother meet every Wednesday to look at books. But who is teaching whom to read?

Wilfrid Gordon McDonald Partridge
by Mem Fox

A child helps an old man in a nursing home find his lost memory.

CHAPTER 6

Loyalty

Before You Begin

The Forgotten Value

Once upon a time, there was a value called loyalty. Loyalty enjoyed a place of high honor in the land. The people of the land respected loyalty. They cherished loyalty, and all that loyalty stood for: love of family, respect for the land, equality, and integrity.

But as time passed, loyalty developed a bad name. The people of the land began to question the necessity of loyalty. They decided that loyalty was stifling and uncool. They abused the value of loyalty, using it to promote their own causes. They twisted loyalty into a reason for deceit. Soon, loyalty was no longer seen as a value, but as a vice. The value of loyalty declined and was replaced by defiance, disdain, scorn, and contempt. Loyalty was not welcome anymore.

But loyalty would not run and hide. Loyalty refused to curl up and die. Even when the people mocked and ridiculed loyalty, loyalty remained faithful and true.

In time, the people again took notice of loyalty. They saw how loyalty kept steadfast and true, even when it was neglected and misused. One by one, the people decided that loyalty was a value they all needed. Loyalty regained its place of honor.

Loyalty is the forgotten value. Once viewed as the core of family and community, loyalty has taken a beating over the years. True, the value of loyalty has often been used in inappropriate ways. Gangs advocate loyalty at all costs, even when it results in violence and, conversely, betrayal. Loyalty is also misused as an excuse for lying. These abuses have made loyalty a value that is often ignored or scorned.

Thankfully, loyalty is regaining its rightful place among values that are integral to healthy families and thus to healthy societies. There will never be a better time than now to promote loyalty as it is meant to be—the key to commitment, dependability, and fidelity. May loyalty be a value that is never forgotten!

LOYALTY

☐ love of family
☐ respect for the land
☐ equality
☐ integrity

To the Family

Dear Family:

A family that is loyal supports, encourages, and defends the other members. The loyal family provides a place where uniqueness is cherished while unity is also of great value. The loyal family allows its members the freedom to make mistakes in an environment that is safe and loving. How can your family cultivate loyalty?

■ Keep your commitments.

Your home, your job, and your activities all demand your time and energy. Don't take on more than you can handle. There are many good causes, but if you overload your schedule, you will find it difficult to keep your commitments. When you are faithful in keeping your promises, you teach your children that loyalty to your responsibilities is important.

Children can get lost in the shuffle of demands on our time. If you promise your child that you'll be on time to her soccer game, keep that promise. Dependability breeds trust, and trust promotes loyalty.

■ Whenever possible, attend each other's special events.

Making each other a priority goes a long way in enhancing loyalty to the family. Do your best to attend the events that are important to the other family members. You may not have much interest in ballet, but if your child is taking ballet lessons and participates in a dance recital, bring the whole family. The support you show is well worth the time.

At the same time, be sensitive to the capacity of very young children and infants to stay quiet for only a short time. Bring a toy or book along to entertain your toddler. If the recital is scheduled for your baby's nap time, find a baby-sitter. A squalling infant is distracting to you and to the people around you.

If you cannot attend the recital, tell your child how proud you are. "Ramona, I sure wish I could be at your recital tonight. I'd much rather be there than at my meeting. But this meeting is one I have to run. Let's go out for an ice cream tomorrow, and you can tell me all about it. I want to hear everything!"

■ Celebrate your family heritage.

Children love to hear stories about when you were a child. Stories of their ancestors can be retold time and again, without children becoming bored.

Is there someone in your extended family that is interested in genealogy? Even if there isn't, you can talk with older members of the family and ask them to tell you what life was like when they were growing up. Record the stories or write them down. Create a family scrapbook that includes old photos, anecdotes, and stories.

Make a family tree. On a large sheet of posterboard, draw a tree trunk with lots of branches. Fill in the names of as many family members as you can on separate leaves. When a new child is born into your extended family, add that name on a new leaf. Take time to look at the tree together and to share what you remember about the people on the tree.

Reward the entire family for acts of loyalty.

Susie defends Garret when a neighbor calls him a crybaby. Celebrate this showing of loyalty by rewarding the entire family with a special treat, a trip to the park, or even just a group rendition of "Hip! Hip! Hooray!"

If you reward the family as a whole, you will lessen the possibility of rivalry, especially between siblings. Only rewarding Susie makes Garret even more the victim. When everyone joins together in celebrating Susie's loyalty, the whole family benefits.

Take turns playing the role of another family member.

Would you like to be a child again, just for an hour? No doubt your child will love being the parent for a change! Switch roles for a set period of time. Put yourself in the other person's shoes.

When you reverse roles, you learn how it feels to be the child, or the parent. This can be quite enlightening! Yet in a very genuine way, empathy and understanding are the glue that cements the bonds of loyalty among family members.

Write a family Pledge of Allegiance.

Work together in designing a family pledge. It can be as simple as, "I will be true to my family, and do whatever I can to look out for the people I love." Memorize the pledge, and recite it at least once a week. Reciting the pledge together can be a great way to start each day!

Each of us will be faced with situations that test our loyalty to all the values that we hold dear. When this happens, take time as a family to talk over these situations and to assure one another that loyalty includes forgiveness and understanding.

Let's Get Started!

Justin's best friend was his dog, Rags. Rags loved Justin, and Justin loved Rags. Whenever Justin wasn't feeling well, Rags curled up next to Justin's bed and stayed by Justin all day long. When Justin came home after being away, Rags wagged his tail so hard he nearly fell over. No matter what, Rags treated Justin as if he were the most special boy on Earth. Which he was, to Rags.

Do you have a friend like Rags? a pet, perhaps, or a member of your family? someone who is loyal to you, even when you're having a bad day? How about you? Are you loyal to your family? your friends? your neighborhood?

Loyalty is a word we don't hear very often. But it is a very important value. When you are loyal to your family, you treat everyone with kindness and respect, two other important values! When you are loyal to a friend, you stick up for him or her, and you are sensitive to his or her feelings. When you are loyal to your neighborhood, you help keep it free of litter and you watch out for the other people who live in your neighborhood.

Loyalty is a funny word, but it is not at all silly. Loyalty is a value that helps us to know that we are loved. Just remember Rags and Justin. I'll bet that right now, Rags is sitting by the door, loyally waiting for Justin to return!

Fingerplay

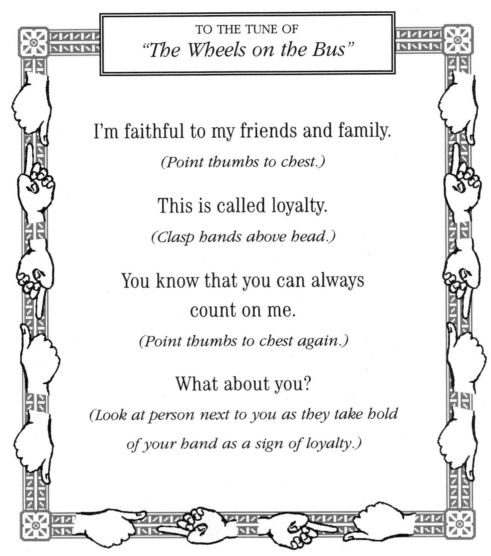

TO THE TUNE OF
"The Wheels on the Bus"

I'm faithful to my friends and family.
(Point thumbs to chest.)

This is called loyalty.
(Clasp hands above head.)

You know that you can always
count on me.
(Point thumbs to chest again.)

What about you?
*(Look at person next to you as they take hold
of your hand as a sign of loyalty.)*

Time for a Story!

When Danielle is invited to go swimming in the pool next door, she finds herself in a tough spot, or a dilemma. She has already promised her brother, Oliver, that she will play with him. What will Danielle do?

Danielle's Dilemma

"Danielle, will you play with me?" Oliver asked his sister.

Danielle liked to play with Oliver. They got along well together. "Sure, Oliver," Danielle said. "I'll be right there." Oliver toddled off to the playroom to get out the action figures. Oliver loved the stories that Danielle made up about his favorite toys.

The telephone rang. Danielle's mother answered. "Danielle, it's for you," she said, handing the phone to Danielle. "It's Mrs. Cosmo next door."

"Hello, Mrs. Cosmo," Danielle said politely.

"It's such a sunny day outside," Mrs. Cosmo said. "I wondered if you'd like to come swim in our pool with Hanna. Baby Sam is taking a nap, and I could watch while you two swim."

"Oh, I'd love to!" Danielle said, then turned to her mother. "Mommy, Mrs. Cosmo is inviting me to swim with Hanna. She said she would watch us. May I go?"

"That would be fine," Mother said. "That's very nice of Mrs. Cosmo to ask you."

"I'll be right over, Mrs. Cosmo. Thank you!" Danielle hung up the phone and ran to her room to get her swimsuit.

When she passed the playroom, Oliver called out to her. "Danielle, I'm ready. Are you going to play with me now?"

Danielle looked at Oliver. He had a big smile on his face. She looked down at her swimsuit. She could almost feel the warm water splashing over her.

"I'm sorry, Oliver. I can't play now. I've been invited to swim at Hanna's pool. When I get back, I'll play with you. Okay?"

continued on page 94

Oliver stared at Danielle and tried not to cry.

After Danielle left, Mother found Oliver curled up in a corner of the playroom. "What's wrong, Oliver?" Mother asked.

"Nothing," said Oliver. He didn't want to tell his mother what had happened because Danielle might get mad at him.

Before Mother could ask Oliver another question, the front door slammed and Danielle came down the hall. She wasn't wet.

"What are you doing home so soon?" Mother asked.

Danielle looked at Oliver. Oliver would not look at Danielle.

"I decided I could swim with Hanna another time," Danielle said. "I promised Oliver I would play with him first. Right now, I want to play with Oliver."

Oliver sat up and grinned. He wiped his eyes on his sleeve, and held out an action figure.

"Here, Danielle," he said, handing her a green-and-orange dinosaur. "Tell me the story about when the giant lizard got caught in a tornado."

Danielle began, "There was a giant lizard, who kept chasing all the little boys and girls. . . ." ■

Discussion Questions

1. Was Danielle being loyal to Oliver when she chose to go swimming?

2. Should Oliver have told his mother what Danielle did?

3. Did Danielle do the right thing when she decided not to swim after all?

4. Do you think that Danielle kept her promise to Oliver?

5. Is being loyal more important than always getting to do what you want to do?

1-2-3 Activities!

The following activities will help reinforce the value of loyalty. Where appropriate, Activity Sheets can be duplicated for each child.

ACTIVITY 1—"LOYALTY LINKS," p. 97–98

Supplies needed:

> Activity Sheets 1 and 2
> crayons
> scissors
> paste or glue

One of the benefits of loyalty is that it helps people feel connected. To enhance this idea, the children will create Loyalty Links.

Activity Sheets 1 and 2 lists a number of instances where loyalty can be shown. There are several blanks for the children to write their own ideas.

Color and cut the sheet into strips, following the dotted lines. Each child makes a paper chain out of the links. The children then connect their links to each other's. In the end, all the links will connect into one large paper chain, which can then be connected to make a circle or strung around the room.

HOME SCHOOL TIP

Let all the family members participate. You can add to the chain by filling out a new link whenever someone in the family demonstrates an act of loyalty.

ACTIVITY 2—"LOYALTY BINGO," p. 99

Supplies needed:

> Activity Sheet 3
> stickers

Ask the children to pick a partner. Each pair has its own Bingo board (Activity Sheet 3). Ask the children to look at the pictures and sentences on the board. Tell them, "If you can tell your partner about a time when you were loyal by doing whatever is listed in one of the squares on the Bingo board, then BINGO! You get to put a sticker on that section of the board. See if you can get three in a row, or better yet, fill the whole board!"

Chapter 6: LOYALTY   95

ACTIVITY 3—"THE LOYAL-TEE," p. 100

Supplies needed:

> Activity Sheet 4
> markers
> stickers
> glitter or sequins, scraps of fabric, trims
> glue
> scissors
> clothesline
> clothespins

A sense of being part of a team helps all the members of the team want to be loyal to one another. Have the children choose a class motto, such as "It's royal to be loyal!" or "You can count on me!" You can give them suggestions or see what they decide on their own.

Write the motto on the tee-shirt outlined on Activity Sheet 4. Children decorate the tee-shirts and cut them out. String a clothesline in the room. When the tee-shirts are finished, hang them on the line with the clothespins. The tee-shirts will be a visible reminder that everyone is part of the same team.

HOME SCHOOL TIP

Use a real tee-shirt. Make up a family motto or use the family name or family nickname (such as "The Bostrom Bunch"), and make shirts for the whole family.

The Value-Able Child Copyright © 1999 Good Year Books

Loyalty

Loyalty Links

Decorate the strips of paper, and then cut them out. Make a paper chain. Connect your chain to the chains of your friends. We are linked together when we are loyal to each other!

I AM LOYAL WHEN I DEFEND MY FRIENDS.

I AM LOYAL WHEN I REFUSE TO LITTER.

I AM LOYAL WHEN I PUT THE NEEDS OF OTHERS BEFORE MY OWN.

I AM LOYAL WHEN I KEEP MY PROMISES.

Loyalty

More Loyalty Links

I AM LOYAL WHEN I TELL THE TRUTH.

I AM LOYAL WHEN I _____

I AM LOYAL WHEN I _____

I AM LOYAL WHEN I _____

ACTIVITY SHEET 2

Loyalty

Name _____

Loyalty Bingo

Pick a partner. Look at the sentences on the Bingo board. If you can tell your partner about a time when you were loyal by doing what is listed on the Bingo board, then BINGO! You get to put a sticker on that section of the board. See if you can get three in a row— or better yet, fill the whole board!

BINGO BOARD

I keep a promise.	I honor my neighborhood.	I support my family.
I consider the feelings of others.	I like myself.	I defend my friends.
I admit when I am wrong.	I look out for people.	I respect my parents.

The Value-Able Child, Copyright © 1999 Good Year Books.

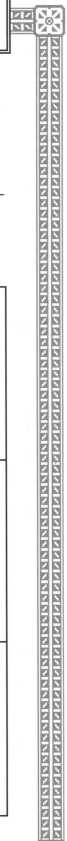

Loyalty

The Loyal-Tee

ACTIVITY SHEET 4

Community Connections

■ **Promote community pride.**

Several of the Community Connections already suggested in this book apply also to the value of loyalty. Loyalty to one's community is promoted through respect for property, both private and public. Focus on children's neighborhoods, a local park, or a library's grounds, and give time to help keep that area free of litter.

■ **Learn your flags.**

The flag is a symbol of loyalty to one's country. Study the flags that represent your state and the other states. Each state has a different flag, yet all of us are united under one flag. Visit a local shop that sells flags or get a book depicting flags of different countries. If your heritage is from another country, find out which flag represents that country.

Have children design their own family flags out of fabric or paper to be hung in their homes. Children could also make flags representing the country of their heritage as well as the country in which they now live, if those are different. We can be loyal to our heritage and to the country of our residence.

■ **Sponsor a community-wide "Loyalty Day."**

Find out the colors of your school, if you don't already know. Talk to the administrators of the school as well as the local government, and declare a community-wide "Loyalty Day." Everyone wears the school colors on that day.

If there is more than one school in your community, combine the colors! If one school's colors are red and black and another uses blue and gold, any combination of those colors can be worn on "Loyalty Day."

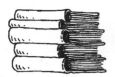

Reading List

Loyalty
published by Golden Books

A basic book for young children describing the value of loyalty

Loyalty: Zach Learns About True Friendship (Adventures from the Book of Virtues, No. 8)
by Shelagh Canning

Following an accident in which Zach breaks a World War II monument, he learns a true story about the meaning of loyalty.

Paperboy
by Mary Kay Kroeger

Despite the lack of interest on the part of the people in his community, a paperboy remains loyal to his job and is rewarded for his faithfulness.

Patrick Loves Peaches: A Story to Help Children Understand Peer Pressure and Loyalty
(from the *Helping Children Understand* series)
by Julie G. Dickerson

This is a picture book that tells how a young boy learns a lesson about peer pressure and what it means to be loyal.

Respect

Before You Begin

The Golden Rule

"Treat others as you wish to be treated yourself." This is the Golden Rule that urges all people to treat one another with dignity and respect.

The value of respect seems to have diminished as the concepts of "if it feels good, do it" and "get ahead whatever the cost" have risen in popularity. Without respect, society, family, and even individuals crumble under the strain of "doing one's own thing."

Respect is often defined as "obedience." In actuality, obedience is but one component of respect; however, the mere following of commands is not respect. While many adults expect or demand obedience from others, especially children, obedience without respect is a poor substitute for cooperation that is borne from true respect between individuals.

Respect requires that we honor one another even when there is disagreement, that we honor our environment, and that we honor ourselves. We respect other people when we believe that their opinions and objectives are valid. We respect our environment when we stand up against pollution and unnecessary damage of the Earth. We respect ourselves when we accept who we are and stop wasting time clinging to our hurts and disappointments.

Picture a scene in a family restaurant. At one table, the Jones family sits together. The children, ranging in ages from five to fourteen, display wonderful manners and appear to be thoroughly enjoying themselves. At another table, the Collick family sits frowning and grumbling, yelling at the waitress, and generally disrupting the other people in the restaurant.

If we could listen in on the two families' conversations, we might hear something like this:

The Jones family: *"Jeremy, would you please pass the salt? Thank you." "Carrie, I'm so proud of how you ordered your own meal." "Oops! It's okay, Bobby, you didn't spill that water on purpose. Let's get our napkins and wipe it up together." "Let me finish hearing what Daddy is telling me, and then it's your turn, Derek." (To the waitress): "You've taken good care of us tonight. Thank you so much!"*

The Collick family: *"How many times do I have to ask you to give me the salt! Now give it to me, now!" "Cindy, you're such a crybaby. Stop it! I'm tired of listening to you." "Shut up, Tom, and let me finish what I'm saying." "You loser! You're always making such a mess. Can't you ever learn?" (To the waiter): "What's taking you so long? We haven't got all night to sit here while you slowpokes take your sweet time!"*

We receive respect when we learn how to give respect—when we follow the Golden Rule and treat others as we wish to be treated. Imagine what the world would be like—or even our own families—if we all consistently followed the Golden Rule.

To the Family

Dear Family:

Respect. The concept of respect has many different implications, depending on how we have been raised. We define *respect* as being able to "treat others as you wish to be treated yourself."

Respect includes honoring parents, elders, and people in authority. It means honoring other people despite your differences and honoring your own self as well. Yet respect involves more than people. Respect for the environment is also important, as is respect for others' possessions, respect for society, and respect for the systems that bind communities and countries together.

Learning respect begins at home. Be a model of self-respect by not criticizing yourself unnecessarily. Adults who constantly put themselves down do not exemplify a sense of respect for self, which is the foundation of respect for others. The challenge in this is also to be able to admit when you've made a mistake! This will show your child that you respect him or her enough to be willing to learn from your own mistakes and to apologize when you're in the wrong.

■ Teach manners by using them yourself!

Say "please" and "thank you," even for the smallest of deeds. Show politeness to the clerk in the grocery store, the postal carrier, the garbage collector. When you receive an irritating phone call from a solicitor, instead of banging down the phone, say, "Thank you for calling, but I'm not interested. Good-by," and hang up. Remind yourself that actions often do speak louder than words!

■ Give reasons for your decisions.

When Molly asks, "Can I have a sleepover Friday night?" and you say no, she's probably going to ask you why not. Answering with "Because I said so!" may be tempting. A more helpful approach would be to give the reason. "We planned to have a family night on Friday because it's been a while since we were all home together for an evening. But let's think of another time soon when you can have a friend spend the night." Even if Molly doesn't agree with you, she will know that you have a good reason for your response and that you respect her feelings enough to tell her that.

■ Listen to your comments about other people.

Saying "That coach is a jerk!" does little to teach a child about respect. Making derogatory comments, even in an off-hand manner, shows a lack of respect for differences in opinions. "I don't agree with the way that coach runs her team," is another way of standing up for yourself without having to put someone else down to do it.

■ Be a good sport.

Nobody enjoys being around a poor sport. You can certainly be disappointed when your daughter's soccer team loses a game, but don't rant and rave about it. That won't change the outcome. Be a good sport! Shake hands with the parents and players on the other team as well as your own. You might surprise a few people, but you may find yourself being an example of respect that others choose to follow.

■ Respect privacy.

Don't read mail that is not addressed to you. Knock before entering your child's room. Allow everyone in the house a "free space" where they can go to be alone. Ask that your children respect your own need for privacy. Everyone deserves 15 minutes of uninterrupted time in the bathtub, at least!

■ Work out a system for an allowance.

Even very young children can learn to respect the value of money. By kindergarten age, a child is quite capable of earning an allowance through simple chores, such as putting out the recyclables or emptying the silverware out of the dishwasher. Children take pride in having their own money. And when you're shopping and your child says, "I want that toy!" you'll find out in a big hurry how much that toy is really wanted if your answer is, "Okay, but you have to use your own money to buy it."

■ Allow choices, while setting boundaries.

Respect your child's opinions, even when you disagree. Be selective about when there's room for negotiation and when there is not. If Marty decides he wants to eat whatever he wants whenever he wants it, you will need to set limits. However, if Marty wants to rearrange the furniture in his bedroom, that is a prime opportunity to allow him some freedom in making a choice. Listen to what he has to say before you chime in with your opinion, "No, that won't work." If you respect your child's opinions, your child will learn to respect yours.

Boundaries and limits have to be set and enforced. Nobody enjoys being with children who are demanding and who get their own way all the time. Giving in to every request does not teach respect—it teaches selfishness, and that is not of value to anyone.

True respect goes hand in hand with the other values we are learning about this year. As families learn to give and earn respect, all the other values will be enhanced as well. Everyone is a winner!

Let's Get Started!

Have you ever heard of the Golden Rule? "Treat others as you wish to be treated yourself." This is what respect is all about.

If somebody calls you a bad name, does that make it okay for you to do the same? Absolutely not! Refusing to call people bad names is one way of showing your respect—for yourself and for the other person.

When your friend throws litter on the ground, should you throw litter too? Of course not! Taking good care of the Earth is another type of respect that is very important. Imagine what would happen if everybody in the world stopped using trash cans. Soon, there would be no room left for anybody to walk!

How does it feel when you are talking and somebody interrupts you? Interrupting somebody else is not a way of showing respect, but taking turns is.

Respect is one of the ten values we are learning about. There are many types of respect: respect for other people, respect for the world, and respect for yourself. That's right—yourself. It's important for you to believe that you are a wonderful person and that you have lots of good ideas. In fact, I'm going to ask you to tell me about some of those ideas. Let's make a list of classroom (or house) rules that helps us remember ways we can show respect. (Write the ideas on a large sheet of posterboard, to leave in the room. Number the rules. When somebody breaks one of the rules, you can say, "Remember Rule 2! Now, try again.")

Possible Rules:

• Always raise your hand when you want to speak, and wait to be called upon.

• Say "please" and "thank you."

• Never call anybody a bad name.

• No pushing or shoving.

• No littering.

• Take turns.

Remember, always treat others the way you want to be treated. Let's practice our fingerplay together.

The Value-Able Child, Copyright © 1999 Good Year Books.

Fingerplay

TO THE TUNE OF
"Twinkle, Twinkle, Little Star"

R - E - S - P - E - C - T,

(Count off seven fingers.)

Treat the world as family.

(Hold arms above head in a circle.)

Be polite in every way,

(Hold hands together.)

What you do and what you say.

(Touch mouth.)

R - E - S - P - E - C - T,

(Count off seven fingers.)

Taking care of you and me.

(Hug self.)

Time for a Story!

Robert doesn't seem to know the meaning of respect. But when he plays with his friend next door, he discovers that it's much more fun to treat other people the way he wants them to treat him.

Rude Robert

"Oh, no!" said Allie, looking out the window of her house. "Here comes Robert!"

Allie, Evan, and Michael stared at each other. What should they do? They didn't like it when Robert came to play. He always broke one of their toys or got into a fight.

Knock! Knock! Knock! Robert was at the door. "Come in, Robert," said Allie.

"I want to play with Evan's cars," Robert said, pushing Allie aside. Robert marched off to Evan's room and pulled a box out from under his bed. He dumped the box of cars on the floor before Evan could say a word.

Robert began racing the cars over the carpet. The wheel of one car broke off. "Oh well," Robert said. "You have lots of other cars."

He left Evan's cars dumped on the floor. "Hey, Michael!" Robert called. "You want to draw some pictures?"

"Sure," Michael said. Michael loved to draw. He brought out a box of colored pencils and his new sketch pad.

Michael worked carefully on a drawing of his dog, Ruffles. "That's a stupid picture," Robert said, looking at Michael's paper. Then Robert crumpled up his picture and threw it on the ground. "I'm tired of this," he said. "I'm going to go play with Allie."

Allie was out in the yard, checking the new green sprouts that had grown from the flower seeds she had planted the week before. Before she knew it, Robert bent over and pulled several sprouts from the ground.

continued on page 111

"Hey!" Allie said. "Why did you do that? Those are my flowers!"

"Big deal," said Robert.

After Robert finally left, Allie, Evan, and Michael met in Allie's room. "We have to do something about Robert," Allie announced.

"He breaks my toys!" said Evan.

"He's rude!" said Michael.

"What can we do?" Evan asked.

"I have an idea," Allie said. The three children got a piece of paper and wrote down their plan.

The next day, Robert returned. Knock! Knock! Knock! He opened the door before any of the children had a chance to answer.

Allie met him in the hall. "Go back outside and knock again," she said. "And don't come in until I open the door."

Robert looked surprised, but he did as Allie said.

When Allie opened the door and let Robert in, he saw a big poster on the wall. It said "Rules of the House."

"What's this?" he asked, pointing to the poster.

"Those are our rules," Michael said. "If you want to play at our house, you have to follow the rules."

"Rule Number One," said Allie. "Knock before entering any room."

Robert started to walk off. "Rule Number Two," said Evan. "No playing with any toys unless you ask the owner first. And Rule Number Three: If you break a toy on purpose, you have to pay for it."

"Who's going to make me?" said Robert with a frown.

"Those are the rules," said Evan. "If you don't like them, you can go home."

Robert didn't want to go home. He got lonely being by himself. "Okay," he said to Evan. "Can I play with your cars?"

"Yes," said Evan. "Thank you for asking first. But remember Rule Number Three!"

When Robert and Evan finished playing with the cars, Robert got up. "Rule Number Four," said Evan. "Pick up the toys when you're finished."

Robert reluctantly helped put the cars back in the box.

"Thank you for your help, Robert," Evan said.

Robert started feeling less cranky. He went to Michael's room, where Michael, as usual, was drawing. Robert knocked on the door. "Can I come in?" he asked.

"Sure," said Michael. "Would you like to draw with me?"

"OK," Robert said. "What are you drawing?"

Michael held up the picture of Ruffles. "This is a picture of my dog, Ruffles. I think it's a pretty good drawing, don't you?"

"Yes, it is really good," Robert answered, then waited a moment. "I wish I could draw as well as you," he said. "My pictures never turn out right."

"If you'd like, I'll help you," Michael said.

"Thanks!" said Robert.

Michael showed Robert how to draw the body of a dog. "Now, you try," he said to Robert.

continued on page 112

Chapter 7: RESPECT   111

Robert's picture didn't look anything like Michael's. "See what I mean," he said. "I'm no good at this."

"Your picture is just fine, you just need more practice," Michael said.

"You mean that?" Robert asked.

"Yes, I do," said Michael. "If you'd like another drawing lesson tomorrow, I'd be glad to help."

"Thanks, Michael, that would be great," said Robert, who was feeling better and better.

Robert found Allie reading a book. "What are you reading?" he asked.

"A book about flowers," she answered. "Look at this picture. This is what my flowers will look like in a few more weeks."

"Wow!" Robert said, looking at the bright picture. "I'm sorry I pulled up some of your sprouts yesterday." He looked at the ground.

"I forgive you," Allie said. "But please don't do it again."

"I won't," Robert said.

"If you help me take care of my garden, I'll let you plant some seeds too," Allie said to Robert.

"Can I plant any kind of seed I want?" Robert asked with excitement. Allie nodded her head. "I want to plant pumpkin seeds!" Robert said, clapping his hands. "I'll grow enough pumpkins for all of us."

Evan and Michael walked into the room. "We are all forgetting about Rule Number Five," Evan said.

"Oh, no, not another rule!" Robert said, but not rudely. "What is Rule Number Five?"

"Share with your friends!" Allie, Michael, and Evan said together. Michael ran into the kitchen and brought out a plate full of cookies. "Will you share these cookies with us, Robert?" Michael asked.

"Thank you," said Robert. "I like that rule the best!" ■

Discussion Questions

1. Why do you think Robert was so rude?

2. Would Robert have been nicer if Allie, Evan, and Michael had been rude to him?

3. If Robert had refused to follow the Rules of the House, what should the children have done?

4. What rules do you have at your house about how you treat other people?

5. By the end of the story, Robert felt much better. Why?

1-2-3 Activities!

The following activities will help children learn the value of respect. Where appropriate, Activity Sheets can be duplicated for each child.

ACTIVITY 1—"PLEASE AND THANK YOU," p. 115

Supplies needed:

> Activity Sheet 1
> one baseball cap
> one large whistle
> a large room or outdoor playground
> masking tape or duct tape

"Please and Thank You" is a game similar to "Mother, May I?" This is a good game to play in a large area, such as an outdoor playground or indoor gymnasium, with ten children at a time. The other children can play other games while they are waiting their turn, which helps reinforce the value of respect!

Mark off two lines with the tape, about 20 feet away from each other. Choose one leader. The leader wears a baseball cap, has a large whistle, and stands behind one of the lines. The rest of the children line up in a row behind the other line.

The leader calls out one of the items on the list (see Activity Sheet 1). The first child to give the missing polite word: "*Please* pass the butter," "*Please* move over," or the correct reply "*Thank you for the present*," gets to take one giant step forward. The game continues until one of the children makes it to the finish line.

Object of the game: to learn respectful responses to everyday situations and to make sure that every child gets a turn as leader.

ACTIVITY 2—"MATCH THE SENTENCE, " p. 116

Supplies needed:

> Activity Sheet 2
> pencils or crayons

The object of this game is for the children to match the beginning sentence with the response that shows respect for another person, for the environment, and for one's self. After the children finish the Activity Sheet, discuss their answers. See what other examples the children can come up with on their own.

ACTIVITY 3—"LITTERBUGS," p. 117

Supplies needed:

> Activity Sheet 3
> colored pencils or crayons
> a small plastic trash can
> glue
> scissors

On Activity Sheet 3 there are pictures of a variety of litterbugs. Have the children color the litterbugs and cut them out. Have each child glue one of their litterbugs on the trash can. This is now the litterbug can. Place the can in a prominent place in the room.

Let the children take turns naming instances that show disrespect (calling someone a name, forgetting to say "thank you," breaking a toy on purpose, dropping litter, walking across a neighbor's front lawn, and so on). Go around the room and let each child have one turn before any child gets to answer twice. This is part of learning respect—raising hands and taking turns. When it is a child's turn, after she gives a suggestion, she gets to place a litterbug in the trash can.

Talk to the children about how showing disrespect is like littering—it hurts, just as littering hurts the Earth. We need to be careful that what we say or do doesn't "bug" somebody else.

Let the children keep extra litterbugs. When somebody is rude, the child can hand them a litterbug. The rude person has to correct the behavior before throwing the litterbug in the litterbug can.

Respect

Name _____

Please and Thank You

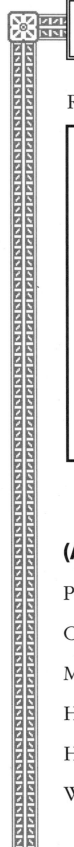

Room setup:

LEADER

(FINISH LINE)

(START LINE)

X   X   X   X   X   X   X   X   X   X

(X = CHILD)

ACTIVITIES FOR LEADER TO CALL OUT

(Add a polite word.)	**(Give the correct reply.)**
Pass the butter.	Here's a present for you.
Open the door.	I made your favorite dinner.
Move over	I made this card for you.
Hand me that book.	I'm taking you to the movies.
Help me with this.	I found the toy you were looking for.
What time is it?	

Name _____

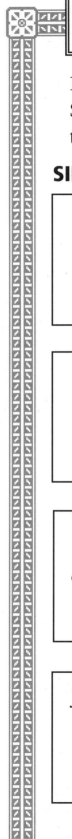

Match the Sentence

Draw a line from the sentence on
Side A to the sentence on Side B
that best completes the sentence.

SIDE A

| I walk up to my neighbor's yard and . . . |

| Peggy and Travis reach the door at the same time and . . . |

| Mr. Derby asks a question in class. I know the answer so I . . . |

| Jill doesn't like the green beans she is served at a friend's house, so she says . . . |

SIDE B

| . . . "get those off my plate!" |

| . . . walk on the sidewalk instead of the grass. |

| . . . shout it out! |

| . . . stomp on the flowers. |

| . . . push each other out of the way. |

| . . . no, thank you. |

| . . . raise my hand. |

| . . . Peggy lets Travis go first. |

ACTIVITY SHEET 2

Name _____

Litterbugs

Community Connections

Respect is a value that is needed in our communities. As we learn to respect ourselves and one another, it is also a logical outreach to be respectful of the places where we live. Encourage children to think up their own ways of showing respect within their community.

■ Adopt a park or piece of land.

Families, classrooms, or other groups can adopt a small piece of land, such as a roadside or park. It is the group's responsibility to keep this area clean by clearing it of litter, picking weeds, and so on. Ask the community to erect a sign at the area's boundaries that says "We Respect Our Community."

Safety Note: Be sure that children are aware of safety rules when near a roadside.

■ Sponsor a class on manners for people of all ages.

Arrange through a social worker or other person to teach a class on manners. The class could include such topics as how to shake hands and greet people, how to treat property that belongs to others (library books and parks, for example), when to say "please" or "thank you," how to behave in a restaurant or public place, how to welcome a new neighbor to the community, and so on.

■ Hold a community clean-up day.

This is different from "adopt a park or piece of land" in that one day is set aside in the spring and in the fall for a community-wide cleanup day. Such an activity might be arranged through the park district, a homeowner's association, or the city government. The idea is for everyone to pick up trash, clean up his or her family's yard, sweep, rake leaves, plant flowers, or do whatever else is needed.

Arrange help for people who cannot do their own work: the elderly, a person with a disability, a single parent, a family where both parents (or the single parent) has to work. In this way, we show respect for property and for the needs of others at the same time!

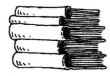

Reading List

The Patchwork Quilt
by V. Flournoy

Tanya learns the story of her family by helping her grandmother patch together a quilt.

Osa's Pride
by Ann Grifalconi

A grandmother teaches her granddaughter about the harmfulness of pride.

Inch by Inch
by Leo Lionni

A charming inchworm learns that respect for his own abilities and the power of other animals can save his life.

Smoky Night
by Eve Bunting

This book tells the story of the Los Angeles riots and the dangerous effects of anger and violence on people's lives and the community.

CHAPTER 8

Self-Control

Before You Begin

Learning to Set Boundaries

"Get control of yourself!" "Pull yourself together!" "Get a grip!" These phrases, usually uttered out of impatience or exasperation, have been said or heard by people of all ages. While some people seem well-equipped to handle their emotional outbursts in a constructive way, others have found that losing control is an effective way to get others to give in to their demands.

The first step in learning self-control is to recognize when it is possible and when it isn't. Two-year-old children cannot be expected to speak rationally about how they feel. Their anger is often expressed in uncontrolled outbursts. However, the nine-year-old who lashes out in destructive anger over any incident may be crying out for help. Nobody enjoys being with people who are out of control, but it is even more uncomfortable to be the person who can't "get a grip."

Children need boundaries. They need limits set on what behavior is appropriate and what is not. It is the job of parents and other adults to set limits for children who are too young to do this for themselves. Ultimately, the goal should be to teach children to learn how to set their own limits, to accept that the world won't always give in to their demands, and to find appropriate ways to express themselves—ways that won't cause harm to themselves or to other people.

The person who has learned self-control is a person who is likely to feel more positive about who he or she is. Being out of control is frustrating and frightening. Learning self-control includes learning to postpone certain self-oriented demands. It includes setting goals and working toward those goals, even when those goals have to be restructured along the way. The person who has a healthy ability to make choices and to be responsible for those choices will ultimately find more satisfaction in life than the person who feels perpetually out of control.

Self-control has its negative drawbacks. It can be used to stifle emotions that need to be expressed. An individual with a healthy degree of self-control is able to express emotions appropriately, but not by using emotions to control the behavior of other people.

In other words, learning self-control is a huge task! Yet, when successful, self-control leads to healthy self-esteem, respect of others, and more positive interactions all around. That's a goal worth seeking!

To the Family

Dear Family:

Teaching children self-control can seem like a full-time job. Some days, the effort may take more energy than we have. That doesn't count the times we're feeling out of control of ourselves. Combine an out-of-control child and an out-of-control adult, and you get a scenario that goes something like this:

Adult: "It's time for bed."

Child: "No."

Adult *(voice rising):* "I said, it's time for bed, NOW!"

Child *(voice also rising):* "NO!"

Adult *(out of control):* "GET TO BED RIGHT NOW OR YOU'RE IN BIG TROUBLE!"

Child *(out of control too):* "I'M NOT GOING TO BED, AND YOU CAN'T MAKE ME!"

You get the picture.

Fortunately, learning self-control is not impossible. Difficult, yes; impossible, no. Like everything else that's important for children to learn, self-control takes effort, consistency, and a lot of patience. A good dose of humor can also help! The person who knows how to exercise healthy self-control is a happier, more confident person. Isn't that worth the work?

■ Designate a special "Get a Grip" corner.

The "Get a Grip" corner can be a small space in a child's room, an area in the den, or any place that is easily accessible and not in a place where the child will draw a lot of attention. When children are having a tough time getting control of themselves, send them to the "Get a Grip" corner. In that corner (which doesn't have to be a corner), a child is allowed to yell, stomp, and work out frustration. Once the child "gets a grip," he or she can come out of the "Get a Grip" corner and resume interaction with the rest of the family.

The "Get a Grip" corner can include paper cups to stomp on or scrap paper to scrunch up. Allowing a child to release frustration in a physical way that doesn't hurt anyone may help the child calm down. It also gives the message that there are both appropriate and inappropriate times and places for expressing anger and frustration.

The adults can use the "Get a Grip" corner too, or make one of their own!

■ Allow children to express their feelings.

Everyone gets angry, and it's an emotion that needs an outlet. Young children may have trouble verbalizing their rage, so it's important that they learn how. Allow your children to say, "I'm angry with you because you won't buy me that toy." It doesn't mean you have to give in and buy the toy. Instead, respond with, "It's fine that you are angry with me, but I am still not going to buy the toy." The child learns that anger is normal, but that anger should not be used to intimidate others.

■ Everybody makes mistakes.

Nobody's perfect. We all make mistakes. But mistakes can be tools for learning. If your child bursts out in a rage or breaks something in anger, you can help your child gain control by being a calming presence. There's no point in trying to reason with an irrational, angry six-year-old! Once the child is settled down, you can discuss what happened. "You broke Jeremy's toy. What should you do about that? You will have to earn the money to buy a new toy or give Jeremy something that belongs to you." Then, when a decision is made, add, "What might be a better way to express your anger next time?"

■ Set limits and follow through.

A child does not like being out of control any more than adults do. Yet young children do not have the capacity to set their own limits in all situations. They will learn limits by having these limits reinforced by an adult who can stay in control. When you tell your child, "If you use that word again, you will not be allowed to watch TV tonight," you will have to follow through or the next time your limits will be meaningless. Be careful not to make threats that you can't keep. Telling a child, "One more bad word and you don't get dessert for a month!" may be impossible to enforce.

Children need limits! It gives them a sense of security and well-being. Whenever possible, set the limits using positive language. "Don't walk on the wet floor" can be rephrased as "You can walk on the floor after it is dry." Even such small examples of positive speech can make the limits you set less likely to cause rebellion.

■ Praise your children!

Catch your child doing the right thing. "Jack, I am proud of the way you stopped yourself before you threw the ball at the cat." Praise their restrained behavior, as well as their positive actions. The child who learns to be proud of exercising self-control will be more apt to keep trying rather than to give in to poor behavior in order to obtain their goals.

■ Oops!

It's late at night, and you're overly tired. Katie accidentally drops a glass of water and you lose control and yell at her. You're only human, after all.

What can you do? Apologize! "Katie, I'm sorry I yelled at you, but I was so tired I lost my temper. Next time, I'll try not to get so angry." When you can admit your own mistakes, it helps your child do the same without shame.

The child who learns constructive ways to vent his or her feelings and to exercise self-control will grow into an adult who is sensitive and confident. Those are two gifts that will last a lifetime.

Let's Get Started!

Let's play an imagination game.

Imagine that you have been playing outside on a hot day. You are very, very thirsty. You run into the house to get a cold drink. "Daddy," you say to your father, "can I have something to drink?"

"Wait until I finish wiping off the table," he says. But you don't want to wait. You are thirsty now! You throw a temper tantrum! Is this the best way to get what you want?

It is hard to be patient when we want something. When things don't go the way we want them to go, it's easy to get angry or frustrated. Exercising self-control in these situations is the goal that we'll be aiming for now.

Exercising self-control! That sounds as if we should be doing jumping jacks or relay races. When we do physical exercise, we build the muscles in our bodies. Doing one sit-up isn't going to keep us in good shape. We have to exercise over and over. We have to practice.

A professional athlete works hard exercising and practicing. And that's just what we're going to do. Only we are going to exercise our self-control muscles. The more we practice self-control, the easier it will be.

How about it? Are you ready for some self-control sit-ups? positive push-ups? You can do it, team!

For our warm-up, let's bend our fingers and learn our new fingerplay!

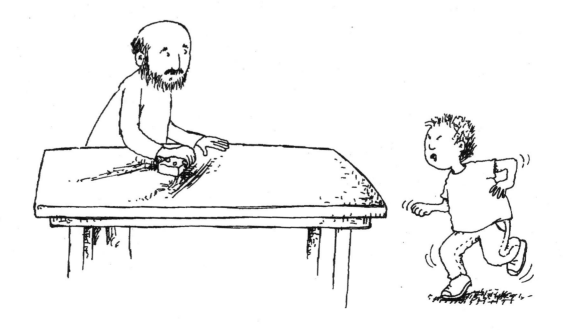

Fingerplay

TO THE TUNE OF
"This Old Man"

Self-control! Self-control!

(Point thumbs to chest.)

Everyone should have this goal.

(Hold arms up like a goal post.)

We will do our best to try and
keep our cool,

(Wipe forehead.)

As we learn to use this tool.

(Pound like a hammer.)

Time for a Story!

Every time Nellie wanted something, she begged and nagged until she got her way. "Please!" she would whine and nag over and over and louder and louder. And it worked! Nellie always got whatever she wanted. Finally, Nellie's family had had enough. They decided it was time for Nellie to find a better way to ask for what she wanted. Can you guess what they did?

Nagging Nellie

Nellie pointed at the stuffed kitten on the shelf at the store. "I want that kitten!"

"No, Nellie, not today," her mother answered.

"Please, Mommy, please!" Nellie nagged. "I want that kitten." And she kept repeating herself over and over and louder and louder.

"Shhhhh!" Nellie's mother said, embarrassed by her behavior. "If you quiet down, I'll buy you the toy."

"Okay, Mommy," Nellie said, smiling. She left the store holding her brand-new toy.

When they got home, Nellie wanted a snack. She opened the cupboard and saw a bag of potato chips.

"It's almost dinner time," her father said. "Can't you wait until we eat?"

"But Daddy, I'm hungry now! Please, Daddy, please, can't I have some potato chips?" And Nellie kept repeating herself over and over and louder and louder.

"Okay, okay, just stop your nagging!" her father said, handing her the bag of chips.

"Thank you, Daddy," Nellie said, grabbing the bag.

After she ate all the potato chips, Nellie ran upstairs to show her new toy to her brother, Jared.

continued on page 128

Nellie found Jared working on a jigsaw puzzle. Nellie had never seen the puzzle before. The puzzle looked like much more fun than her stuffed kitten.

"Can I help?" she asked Jared.

"No, Nellie," Jared said. "I want to do this myself."

"Please, Jared, please!" Nellie whined.

Jared pushed the puzzle pieces toward her. "Go ahead," he said, and left the room.

Nellie moved the puzzle pieces around with her finger. The puzzle didn't seem like such fun anymore.

"Dinner time!" Father called. Nellie left the puzzle, washed her hands, and joined the rest of the family around the table.

Father picked up a bowl of corn and started to scoop some onto his plate.

"I want some corn," Nellie said.

"I'm taking some corn now, Nellie," Father said.

"Please, Daddy, please! Please give me the corn now!"

"You'll have to wait your turn," Father said. After he took his share, he passed the corn to Jared. Nellie was puzzled.

Next, Jared reached for the chicken. He took a drumstick, Nellie's favorite.

"I want the drumstick, Jared," Nellie said.

Jared ignored her and took the drumstick.

"Please, Jared, please! I want the drumstick!" Nellie nagged over and over and louder and louder.

"Did somebody say something?" Jared pretended not to hear Nellie's nagging. This made Nellie angry.

Nellie turned to her mother. "I want more milk."

"Certainly," Mother said. "As soon as I finish my potatoes."

"Please, Mommy, please!" Nellie nagged over and over and louder and louder.

"I guess you'll have to wait until I finish my chicken too," Mother said.

Nellie couldn't believe it. No matter how much she nagged, no matter how loud she nagged, she wasn't getting what she wanted.

She decided to try something new.

"Please, Mommy, when you're through with your potatoes, can you pour me some more milk?"

"Certainly," Mother said, and stood right up and got the milk.

Nellie thanked her mother. I'll try that again, she thought.

"Daddy, may I have some corn?"

"Jared, pass the corn to Nellie, please," Father said.

"Sure," said Jared. "And if you'd like, Nellie, you can have the drumstick."

"Really?" Nellie said, surprised. "Thank you, Jared!"

From then on, Nellie tried her best not to nag for whatever she wanted. It was hard to have self-control all the time, and there were times when Nellie found it very, very hard not to whine and nag. But with everyone's help, Nagging Nellie became Nice Nellie. ■

The Value-Able Child, Copyright © 1999 Good Year Books.

Discussion Questions

1. Is it fun to always get what you want?

2. Can you think of one reason why your parents might tell you "no" when you wish they would say "yes"?

3. Was Nellie always happy and satisfied once she got her way?

4. How did Nellie's family help her keep her self-control?

5. What do you do when you want something?

1-2-3 Activities!

The following activities will help reinforce the value of self-control. Where appropriate, Activity Sheets can be duplicated for each child.

ACTIVITY 1—"ORDER! ORDER!" p. 132

Supplies needed:

> Activity Sheet 1
> pencils

When our life is in disorder, we feel out of control. One way to exercise self-control is to put our lives in order.

Activity Sheet 1 tells the story of Henry, who is having a bad day. He can't find matching socks, so he loses his temper.

There are six sentences that need to be listed in sequence. Each child can figure out the proper order of the story and place a number in the corner of each panel. Afterwards, have the child tell Henry's story, explaining how Henry "got a grip" and exercised self-control.

The Value-Able Child, Copyright © 1999 Good Year Books.

ACTIVITY 2—"MAKE THE GOAL OF SELF-CONTROL," p. 133

Supplies needed:

> Activity Sheets 2 and 3
>
> scissors
>
> glue or paste

The purpose of Activity 2 is to help children think about options when confronted with a situation where they can either react with anger and frustration or exercise self-control.

On Activity Sheet 2 and 3, a hockey player is trying to make a goal but keeps getting blocked. At the bottom of the page are pictures of hockey sticks and hockey pucks. The child cuts out the sticks and pucks and then uses them to help the hockey player reach the goal of self-control.

Paste a hockey stick on a choice that does not show self-control and a hockey puck on the picture that does show self-control. Once all the choices are made, the child has moved toward the goal. The last hockey puck can be placed in the goal.

ACTIVITY 3—"COUNT TO TEN," p. 135

Supplies needed:

> Activity Sheets 4 and 5
>
> pencils
>
> crayons or colored pencils

Activity Sheets 4 and 5 depict examples of situations where a child can choose ways to use self-control. When children have options, they are better prepared to act properly in a situation where self-control is necessary.

Each example has two possible responses. The child draws a line from the box to the best response. At the bottom of Activity Sheet 5, the child can draw an example of exercising self-control in a particular situation.

Self-Control

Name _____

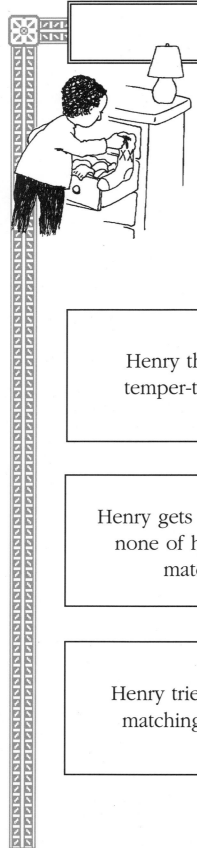

Order! Order!

This story is out of order—just like Henry's life! Help Henry learn self-control and put his day in order.

Number the panels in the order they should go, placing the correct number in the upper left-hand corner. Then, tell Henry's story.

Henry throws a temper-tantrum.	Henry looks in another drawer and finds the missing socks.
Henry gets angry that none of his socks match.	Henry stops the tantrum and counts to ten.
Henry tries to find matching socks.	Henry wakes up.

Self-Control

Name _____

Make the Goal of Self-Control

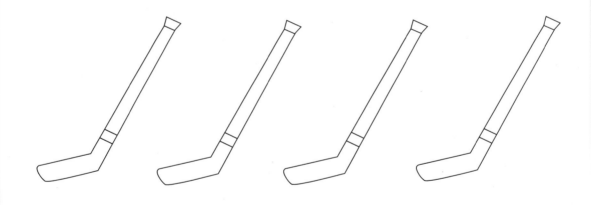

Can you exercise self-control? Try to make the goal of self-control by finding the best way to handle some tough situations.

Cut out the hockey sticks and pucks at the bottom of this page. Paste the hockey sticks on top of the wrong answers, and the pucks on top of the right answers, until you make the goal of self-control.

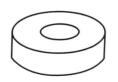 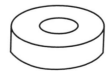  

Self-Control

Name _____

Make the Goal of Self-Control

1 Mom and Dad are talking, but you have something to say. You . . .

a Interrupt.

b Wait your turn.

2 For breakfast, you get to try a new cereal. Everyone wants to go first. You . . .

a Make sure everyone gets a bowl-full.

b Grap the box and pour your bowl-full first.

3 While waiting in line for an ice cream, someone cuts in front of you. You . . .

a Tell the person, "I was here first. Please wait your turn."

b Shove the person out of the way.

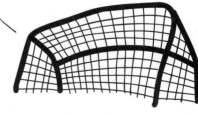

SCORE!

Congratulations! You made the goal of self-control!

Self-Control

Count to Ten

There are many ways we can help exercise our self-control. Match the sentence with the best answer by drawing a line from the box to the answer. Then draw your own idea of how you can exercise self-control in the space provided on the next page.

I am standing in line, getting impatient.

I can count backwards from 100.

I can push and shove.

I see a cake on the kitchen counter.

I can eat some cake.

I can ask permission for a slice.

I am about to lose my temper.

I can scream and yell.

I can draw a picture about why I am angry.

Cooperation

Name _____

Count to Ten

I am sitting behind a girl with a ponytail.	I can sit on my hands. I can pull her hair.
I see a child pushing another child.	I can walk away. I can start pushing too.

Now, you draw your own example of exercising self-control.

The Value-Able Child, Copyright © 1999 Good Year Books.

Community Connections

■ **Take a tour of the local police station.**

Arrange a visit to the local police station. Ask the officers to tell the children how important it is to learn self-control, since many problems are caused when people lose control. For example, if someone is impatient, they may drive too fast and run a red light. This can lead to someone being hurt. Drivers need to exercise self-control and follow the traffic rules.

The officers might also tell the children how the police must exercise self-control. They can explain how difficult it is to keep their self-control when other people are out of control.

■ **Visit a courthouse.**

The idea of this visit is similar to the tour of the police station above. A judge or lawyer can explain to the children how a courtroom works: the people involved, the kinds of cases that come to trial, the outcome of situations where people do not exercise self-control.

You can enact a mock trial, even if you can't visit a real courthouse. Appoint the children to the various roles: judge, lawyer, jury, defendant. Decide on a hypothetical, minor example of something that might happen to a child: Corey got angry and broke a window in his room. Ask: What should the consequences be for this? What could Corey have done with his anger that wouldn't be so destructive?

■ **Talk with a social worker.**

Invite a social worker to discuss with the children ways of exercising self-control, providing examples of coping strategies for dealing with anger, impatience, selfishness, and so on. Include parents in the discussion. Encourage the children to help come up with the answers.

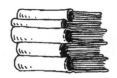

Reading List

The Child's World of Self-Control
by Henrietta Gambill

Illustrations accompanied by simple text portray times when self-control comes in handy.

D.W. Flips!
by Marc Brown

D.W. tries to develop self-control as she practices her forward roll in order to become a great gymnast.

Feelings
by Aliki

Dialogues, stories, poems, and pictures illustrate the range of childhood emotions: love, jealousy, fear, happiness, sadness, and so on.

Sometimes I Feel Like a Mouse
by Jeanne Modesitt

Imaginative text and colorful paintings help children explore their own feelings.

Little Monster Did It!
by Helen Cooper

When Amy's mom leaves for the hospital to have a new baby, she gives Amy a stuffed monster as a present. Little Monster then becomes Amy's vehicle for acting out against the jealousy she feels for the new baby.

On Monday When It Rained
by C. Kachenmeister

Children learn to express their emotions in constructive ways.

CHAPTER 9

Sharing

Before You Begin

Dare to Share

> "That's mine! Give it back!"
>
> "No, I won't! I had it first!"
>
> "I don't have to share with you if I don't want to!"

Ah, the struggle to teach children how to share.

It's not unusual for young children to stake their claims in unyielding and seemingly selfish ways. What's theirs is theirs. Why should they have to share what belongs to them?

Selfishness is not always the motivating factor, although it may appear to be so. Young children are learning what belongs to them. They are learning how to treat their possessions. They are often reluctant to share what they believe is rightfully theirs.

Sometimes that's okay! Children need to know that some of their belongings are theirs, and theirs only. Forcing an older child to always share her toys with a younger sibling may breed more resentment than a willingness to share. An older child should be able to protect some of her belongings from being destroyed by little brother. "Brittany, perhaps you can put your books on the shelf where Timmy can't reach them. But would it be okay if the two of you played together with your stuffed animals?" Respecting a child's property while encouraging the child to share gives a good sense of balance and will enhance the ability of that child to become unselfish.

Selfish people are not likable people. On the other hand, we don't want to encourage children to think they must give in to the whims and demands of everyone else. Helping children learn guidelines that enable them to decide when to share and when not to is a goal that is manageable, healthy, and yes, sometimes frustrating, but worth the time and effort.

In this unit on sharing, children will be encouraged to learn boundaries and guidelines so that they know that their decisions about sharing are respected. Although children can be selfish, they can also be extremely generous and giving. Honoring a child's need to set limits while also encouraging and celebrating his or her capacity for joyful sharing is the challenge upon which we will build as we focus on sharing.

To the Family

Dear Family:

"The family that cares for each other, shares with each other." That's our motto for our lesson on sharing. Sharing is a natural outgrowth of truly caring about other people. When we care for one another as families, even at times when we don't get along, we foster an atmosphere where sharing is a response to caring—not a punishment forced upon us by well-meaning adults.

As is true with all important values, parents and adults are their children's best role models. Be willing to practice what you preach. Children raised in a home where sharing is a common occurrence will be more likely to learn how to share with others. In addition, you can:

■ Celebrate, don't compare, acts of sharing.

Accentuate the positive! When you catch your child sharing, affirm that action: "Elaine, I liked the way you shared your cookies with your sister." Avoid making a big deal out of instances when children refuse to share. Telling a five-year-old, "Annie, you are so selfish about sharing your toys! I'm not buying you anything more," does not inspire a child of that age to share. But saying to Annie, "Maybe Yolanda would like to come over and play your new game with you," puts the emphasis on sharing as a positive, rather than a punishment.

■ Make sharing a habit.

Teach your children how to set aside a portion of their allowance to give to a charity or other worthy cause. When you receive a paycheck, that can be the time to give your children their allowance. Designate a regular amount that you save to give away, and help your child set an amount. For instance, if your child receives $1, give the amount in coins. One dime can be put in a special bank, called the "Sharing Bank." Choose a charity, a community project, a church or temple fund, or whatever is important to you and to your child. Enjoy the fun of building up the savings until you reach a certain goal. When you reach that goal, celebrate! "You have saved $10 to help that family who lost their house in a fire. Good for you!" Your child will not only learn how to save, but will experience the delight in helping others.

■ Use a "talking stick."

Learning to share time and attention is sometimes a more difficult lesson than learning to share actual resources. All children need to know that there are times when they have their parents' undivided attention and there are times when that attention is shared.

Make a "talking stick." You can find a piece of smooth wood and decorate it if you wish. During a meal, or another specified time, take turns passing the "talking stick" around. When one person is holding the "talking stick," everyone else has to keep quiet and allow the person to finish what he or she needs to say. If necessary, set a time limit for how long a person can hold on to the stick. Then pass it to the next person.

Children can also use the "talking stick" when they need to talk to parents about a concern. When a child brings the "talking stick" to a parent, it is understood the parent will stop and take time to listen. It should also be clear that the stick is used only in this way for something that is very important, not just to ask for a treat or to complain about another family member.

■ Allow your children to have certain items they don't have to share.

We all need to know that there are certain prize possessions that we can keep to ourselves. You may have a glass plate that belonged to your grandmother. It's okay to say that the plate is "off limits" and that you are the only one allowed to use it. Let your children designate a few special items the same way. Make it clear to the rest of the family which possessions are off limits. "Cindy got a new doll for her birthday. This is her special doll. She is the only one allowed to touch it, unless she says otherwise." Children will be more likely to respect the limits others set if their limits are respected in return.

Learning to share is a reward in itself. The joy of playing together, sharing your time and possessions, respecting the rights of others, and giving freely just because you want to makes everyone's life a little brighter.

Let's Get Started!

Okay, everybody! I have a challenge for you. I'm calling it "Dare to Share."

Sharing is one of our values. It's easier for us to share when our friends and family are willing to share with us. In the same way, if we are good at sharing, we make it more fun for other people to learn how to share too. That's why I'm challenging you to "Dare to Share."

When we "Dare to Share" we do the following.

- We offer to share a toy or book that is special to us.
- We share our time with one another.
- We let everyone have a turn at sharing.

When we "Dare to Share," we don't say to our friend, "You share those crackers with me or else!" We say, "Would you like to share my snack today? I brought enough for two."

When we "Dare to Share," we share with others because we want to, not because we want something back in return.

When we "Dare to Share," we look for ways to share. Do you have a neighbor who lives alone? The next time you bake cookies at home, make an extra batch to give to your neighbor. Your neighbor will be happy and you will be too. Life is much more fun when we all share.

When we "Dare to Share," we're teaching other people to dare to share too. Let's show everyone how much we care, because we "Dare to Share."

Fingerplay

TO THE TUNE OF
"Row, Row, Row Your Boat"

Share, share, share, our toys

(In a circle, pretend to pass toys around.)

That's what makes life fair.

(Repeat.)

Dare to care and also share,

(Repeat.)

At home and everywhere.

(Hold out both hands as if holding something.)

Time for a Story!

Derek is proud of the baseball he caught at the ball game last weekend. All his friends want to play with it. Derek doesn't want to share. How will his friends respond?

Mine—All Mine!

Every year, on the first day of the baseball season, Derek's Uncle Corey took him to a ball game.

Derek wore his baseball cap. Uncle Corey bought Derek a hot dog and a bag of peanuts. Nobody cared if Derek threw the empty peanut shells on the ground.

Derek and Uncle Corey always brought their baseball mitts to the game, hoping they would catch one of the home run balls. A few balls had come close, but Derek and Uncle Corey had never caught one.

This was Derek's lucky year. In the third inning, one of the players on the home team hit a home run. The ball sailed high in the air, then fell down, down, down, into the bleachers—and right into Uncle Derek's baseball mitt!

"Here you go, champ," Uncle Corey said, tossing the ball to Derek.

"Oh, thank you, Uncle Corey!" Derek said. He held the ball in both hands, smelled the wonderful smell of leather and dirt, and then gave his uncle a big hug.

Derek couldn't wait to show the baseball to his friends. As soon as they returned home, Derek ran to the park across the street where some of his friends were playing.

"Look what I got!" Derek shouted, holding the baseball high in the air.

"Wow!" Jamie said. "Where'd you get that?"

"I caught it at the baseball game today," Derek answered. "Well, actually, my uncle Corey caught it, but he gave it to me to keep."

"Cool!" said Jamie. "Can I see it?"

Derek held the ball out to Jamie, but when she reached for the ball, Derek pulled his hand back.

continued on page 146

"Can't I hold it?" Jamie asked, puzzled.

"No," said Derek. "This baseball is mine—all mine."

Jamie walked away.

Next, Alex held out his hand. "What about me? I'm your best friend. Can I hold your baseball?"

"No," said Derek. "This baseball is mine—all mine."

"Well, then, you can have it," Alex said, and ran off to play with Jamie.

Derek stood by himself, staring at the baseball. It's mine!, he thought. I don't have to share it with anyone.

Uncle Corey watched Derek and his friends. He saw Jamie, then Alex, turn away from Derek.

"Hey, there, champ," Uncle Corey said. "You look glum. What's wrong?"

"Nobody will play with me," said Derek.

"Why not?" Uncle Corey asked, although he knew.

"Because I won't let them hold my baseball," Derek answered.

"Why not?" Uncle Corey asked again.

"Because it's mine—all mine," Derek said. "I don't have to share if I don't want to."

Uncle Corey put his arm around Derek's shoulder. "You're right, Derek," he said.

"That baseball is yours. You don't have to share it. But put yourself in Jamie's place. Alex's too. If one of your friends had had a baseball like that, you would want to hold it too."

Derek rubbed the ball on his hand. "You're right," he said. "I guess it wouldn't hurt anything if I let my friends hold the baseball."

"You can let them know they need to be careful, because it is special to you," Uncle Corey said. "If you tell them that and they aren't careful, you can tell them that you won't share the ball again. But I bet they'll be careful."

"Guess what I was thinking," Derek said to his uncle. "I was thinking that if you hadn't shared the ball with me, I wouldn't even have it."

"Aren't you smart!" said Uncle Corey. "It made me happy to share the baseball with you. And you'll be happy to share it with your friends."

"Jamie, Alex!" Derek ran after his friends. "Do you want to hold my baseball?" ■

Discussion Questions

1. How would Derek have felt if Uncle Corey had kept the baseball for himself?

2. Should Jamie and Alex have asked Derek if they could hold his baseball?

3. If Jamie and Alex had grabbed the ball away from Derek, would that have been right?

4. Do we always have to share what belongs to us?

5. What is something you can share with a friend?

1-2-3 Activities!

The following activities will help reinforce the value of sharing. Where appropriate, Activity Sheets can be duplicated for each child.

ACTIVITY 1—"GIFTS THAT KEEP ON GIVING," p. 150

Supplies needed:

> Activity Sheet 1
> crayons or colored pencils
> scissors

Activity 1 teaches children that sharing includes the sharing of time and creativity, as well as the sharing of possessions.

Using Activity Sheet 1, children can choose ways of sharing with family and friends. Printed on the sheet are gift boxes. Have children write on each box, or dictate to you to write, a different type of sharing they can do: "I can share my favorite toy"; "I can share my time"; "I can share a story."

The gift boxes work like coupons. Children cut out and give the coupons to the person of their choosing.

The gift box coupons can be used over and over. Even the recipients of the gifts can give the same gift in return!

ACTIVITY 2—"THE MAGIC PENNY," p. 151

Supplies needed:

> Activity Sheet 2
> crayons or colored pencils
> scissors
> tape player and music cassette

At the top of Activity Sheet 2 is a song about a Magic Penny. The idea is that the more you give, the more you have to give. Sharing is like a Magic Penny. The more we share, the more we want to share, and the more that others will want to share with us.

The pennies can be colored and cut out. Then it's time for the "Magic Penny" game. Everyone sits in a circle. The leader turns on the music. Start passing the pennies around the circle. When the leader stops the music, stop passing the pennies. Everyone should still have at least one penny—maybe more!

After the music is played several times, stop the game and have a discussion. No matter how many pennies you gave away, you kept getting more back. Everyone gave pennies, and everyone received pennies. What kinds of things besides Magic Pennies can you share with others? Ideas can be written on the Magic Pennies.

Another use of the Magic Pennies can be to save them in a Magic Penny bank. Draw a large piggy bank on a sheet of posterboard. Ask the children to let you know when they have shared something. Write the child's "gift" on the penny, and paste it in the bank. As the children share the ways they've shared, the bank will fill up to overflowing!

ACTIVITY 3—"LOOK WHAT I CAN SHARE!" p. 152

Supplies needed:

> Activity Sheet 3
> crayons or colored pencils

Have a class talent show. Everyone who wishes can do a skit, recite a poem, tell a joke, do a trick, or whatever they choose. All of us have talents to share. Celebrate the gifts we share with one another.

Children can draw a picture on Activity Sheet 3 of their special talent. Or, they can draw a picture of another child sharing a talent. The idea is not to compare ourselves with one another, but to rejoice in the sharing of who we are as unique and wonderful individuals.

HOME SCHOOL TIP

If you are teaching one child at home, enlist the whole family to be part of the talent show—or invite your neighbors to join you!

Sharing

Gifts That Keep on Giving

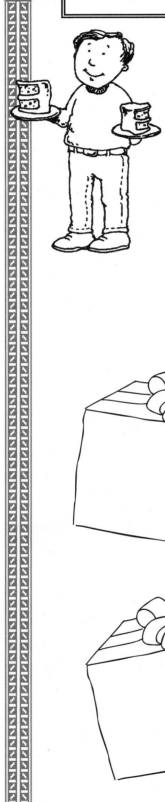

Write on each gift something you can share.
Then cut out the gifts and give them away
to the person you will share with!

Sharing

Name _____

The Magic Penny

*Love is something if you give it away,
give it away, give it away,*

*Love is something if you give it away,
you end up having more.*

*It's just like a magic penny; hold it tight
and you won't have any.*

*Lend it, spend it, and you'll have so many,
they'll roll all over the floor!*

Sharing

Name _____

Look What I Can Share!

Here's something special I can do,
Just watch me, and I'll share with you!

Community Connections

Imagine a community where everybody is eager to share! There would be less hunger, less poverty, less crime, and more resources to go around. A community would be what a community should be: a place where neighbors look out for one another and where harmony outranks hostility.

We can't change the whole world, but we can make a difference in our own communities. Here are a few ways that sharing can be promoted in your community.

■ **Organize a toy or clothing drive.**

Many communities have homeless shelters or shelters for abused women or children. Even if your community doesn't, you can locate these places in other areas. Through your school, Scouting organization, a church or temple, or a similar group help organize a drive to collect toys or clothing. Children gain a great sense of satisfaction when they give to another child who has less. A child can choose a toy that is no longer used or save their money to buy a new toy and give it to a toy drive. Children can also help sort toys or clothes, place them in boxes, and deliver them to a shelter.

In areas of the country where winter is severe, a mitten and hat collection is an affordable way for people to collect items that shelters can give to people in need.

Donate books to a library for a book sale.

As children move from one reading level to the next, many families find they have collected piles of books that are still in good condition. Adults who regularly purchase books to read also may find themselves with stacks of books they'll never read again. Gathering used books and donating them to the local public library or a school library is an activity that both adults and children can do together.

If your local library does not sponsor a book sale, maybe you can get one started! The money raised buys new books for the library, and may bring new patrons to the library. A library is a place where sharing resources is the name of the game!

> **Remember:** When you are giving away clothes, toys, books, or other household items, don't give items that are torn, broken beyond repair, dirty, or trashed. Giving away items that you would not use yourself does not teach children how to share. It teaches children to share only when it is convenient and easy.

Help feed the hungry.

All ages can collect canned food for a local food pantry. Children can decorate paper grocery bags to distribute in neighborhoods and grocery stores for the collection of food. Although the holidays are a popular time to gather food for the hungry, it may be more helpful to collect food at other times of the year, when the needy people in our communities are often forgotten.

Share the gift of your time.

Sharing what you have does not always have to focus on material things. Sharing the gift of time is just as important. Visit a senior citizens center and play games with the residents. Volunteer to take library books to people who cannot leave their homes. Help clean up a local park or forest area. When we share, the emphasis is not on the cost of what we give. Sharing your time is a gift without price.

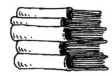

Reading List

Giving
by Shirley Hughes

A little girl lists all the things she gives and receives during the day.

Sam and the Lucky Money
by Karen Chinn

While celebrating the Chinese New Year, Sam discovers a homeless man and his "lucky money" takes on a new meaning.

The Book of Giving: Poems of Thanks, Praise, and Celebration
by Kay Chorao

A collection of more than sixty poems that celebrates the gifts of life.

The Giving Tree
by Shel Silverstein

Throughout a boy's life, a faithful tree keeps giving just what he needs.

The Rainbow Fish
by Marcus Pfister

The Rainbow Fish discovers that by sharing his glittering scales with the other fish, he is no longer the most beautiful fish in the sea—but he is the happiest!

CHAPTER 10

Tolerance

Before You Begin

Keeping an Open Mind and Heart

The Ling family moves to the United States from China. Mr. and Mrs. Ling hope to raise their children in an environment that respects differences in culture and opinion. One morning, they step outside their home and find cruel slogans painted on their garage.

Joe suffers from multiple sclerosis. On his worst days, he is confined to a wheelchair. On these days, he is unable to go to work, because the building that houses his office does not have handicap-accessible doorways.

Jill's favorite cartoon makes fun of people who are overweight. Jill thinks it is funny to call Chad "fatso" when she sees him on the playground. She has no idea how much her "funny" remarks hurt Chad's feelings.

Everywhere we turn, we find ourselves confronted by examples of intolerance. Unfortunately, many of these situations go unnoticed until we are the ones who experience the intolerant attitudes of people and society.

Many schools go out of their way to try to be "fair" to all cultures. One way this has been accomplished is to eliminate or greatly water down mention of any religious holidays. While on the surface this may seem to be a fair solution, it prevents children from learning tolerance through exposure to the fundamental differences in religions and cultures. It is only through valuing the differences between people that tolerance—and dignity—can be achieved.

From an early age, children are faced with examples of intolerance. Being picked on by a bully, ridiculed for a disability, or teased for being different are all instances of intolerance. Children exposed to intolerance often learn to be intolerant. Yet the reverse is also true. Children who are raised in an atmosphere of tolerance learn to be open-minded and understanding of others.

Giving children responsibility aids them in learning to be giving and caring of others. When Carly saves her own money to donate to the homeless during the holidays, she is learning to be tolerant of people in tough situations and to be compassionate as well.

Understanding one another is the key to tolerance. As teachers, parents, leaders, and role models, adults can work with children in defeating the intolerance that breeds contempt and prejudice. Learning and valuing the differences in cultures, races, physical characteristics, education, vocations, and personalities can lead to acceptance and promotion of honor among all people. "Any pain is our pain: That's the root of tolerance," director Steven Spielberg once said.[1] As we seek to "walk in one another's shoes," we will discover how true this statement is.

Our country is founded on the premise that all people are created equal. Children should be raised to be proud of this foundation, which includes being proud of themselves and their uniqueness and proud of all people, whatever the differences among them.

[1] From *Teaching Tolerance,* a publication of the Southern Poverty Law Center, 400 Washington Ave., Montgomery, AL, 36104. Fall 1997, p. 6.

To the Family

Dear Family:

Tolerance is a value that is often best understood by examining instances of its opposite: intolerance.

Children find examples of intolerance every day. Differences in physical appearance, intelligence, race, culture, and religion are often the cause for ridicule and abuse. Adults must be aware of the subtle and the obvious ways in which we allow intolerance to go unchecked. As parents, you can help teach tolerance in the following ways:

■ **Recognize stereotypes and challenge them.**

Cartoons and television often portray overweight people as incompetent, homeless people as lazy, and religious people as fools. When you see a person cast into a stereotype, point it out to your child. Try to use positive examples. For instance, when the boy next door, who is somewhat overweight, wins an award in the science fair, say "George is really smart! Isn't that great about his award?" You do not need to point out that George is heavy. Affirm his positive qualities.

■ **Watch television with your children and discuss any examples of intolerance and prejudice.**

It seems that no matter how hard we try to make sure our children aren't exposed to inappropriate TV programs, unless we keep the TV off, material will sometimes be unsuitable. Take the opportunity (before you shut it off) to talk about what was just viewed. For example, when a TV cartoon character is ridiculed for being different, ask your child, "Is it right to call Jakob names just because he is from another country? If you were Jakob's friend, what would you do?"

■ **Watch what you say!**

Using derogatory names for people or cultures that are different teaches intolerance. Find positive ways to refer to others, and model these at home.

■ Don't criticize the person—correct the action.

When your child exhibits inappropriate behavior, say, "I don't like it when you hit your brother," rather than "You stupid kid!" And likewise, don't call yourself names! Demeaning yourself teaches that it is okay to demean others too.

■ Encourage your children to express their feelings, not to retaliate.

If your child is the victim of a bully or racial slur, explain that it is okay to say to the offender, "I don't like it when you call me that." Reacting with violence or foul talk does little to equip your child to deal with negative situations. If the problem continues, you may need to take more decisive action. Try to work it out with everyone involved.

Tolerance may seem like a difficult value to practice all the time. But the more you do, the more it will be a way of life.

Let's Get Started!

Tolerance is probably not a word you hear very often. Yet, it is a very important value.

Tolerance means lots of different things: not judging other people; accepting the differences in others; refusing to make fun of people that don't look or act like you do; enjoying what makes each person unique and special. When we are tolerant of others, we can take pride in ourselves and in everyone else too.

Can you think of a time when somebody made fun of you or teased you for something that you couldn't help? For instance, you fall and cut your face and have to get stitches. When you get the stitches out, you are left with a scar. One day, as you are walking home, somebody points at you and laughs at your scar. How does that make you feel? You can't help the way you look. Is it right for somebody to make fun of you? No!

A good rule to help you remember to be tolerant is this: "Walk a mile in my shoes." That doesn't mean we should take off our shoes and trade them with our best friend! To "walk a mile" in someone else's shoes means to try and imagine what that person feels like. If we do this, we will be more likely to be tolerant of differences, because we know that being different is okay. In fact, it's very, very good. Wouldn't the world be a boring place if everybody was exactly the same?

We'll be playing some fun games to help us learn about tolerance. In addition, I'd like to hear about times when you have seen people be unkind to someone because he or she was not the same as them. How do you think that made the person feel? How did that make you feel? Would it have helped to have the unkind person walk a mile in the other person's shoes?

We can begin to learn about tolerance by repeating together this cheer:

> *"We're all different—every one—*
> *And that's what makes this world such fun!"*

Try it with me (repeat the cheer). Now, it's on to our fingerplay.

The Value-Able Child, Copyright © 1999 Good Year Books.

Fingerplay

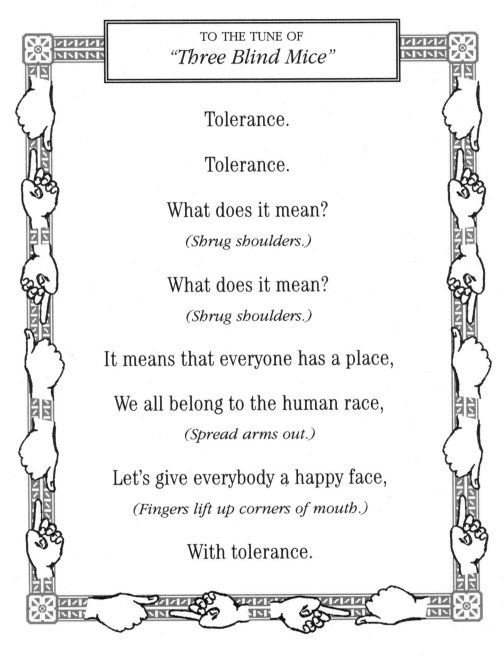

TO THE TUNE OF
"Three Blind Mice"

Tolerance.

Tolerance.

What does it mean?
(Shrug shoulders.)

What does it mean?
(Shrug shoulders.)

It means that everyone has a place,

We all belong to the human race,
(Spread arms out.)

Let's give everybody a happy face,
(Fingers lift up corners of mouth.)

With tolerance.

Time for a Story!

Tolerance *is a word that means being understanding of one another and accepting that differences between people are okay. Todd finds himself in a situation where tolerance—understanding and acceptance—allows him to discover a wonderful new friend.*

Todd's Surprise

Todd and his parents recently moved into a small brick house. Around the corner from Todd's home, an old woman lived alone. The children in the neighborhood were afraid of her. All they knew was that her name was Mrs. Farrell. None of them had ever met her because Mrs. Farrell spent most of her time inside her house or out in her backyard.

One sunny spring day, Todd decided to ride his bike. As he neared the corner where Mrs. Farrell lived, he heard a strange sound. Maybe it's a kitten! Todd

thought. He parked his bike on the side-walk and listened carefully. The sound came from Mrs. Farrell's backyard.

Carefully, Todd tiptoed to the fence, and peeked through. There, in the yard, he saw an incredible sight! It was not a kitten at all. It was Mrs. Farrell, singing, as she cut flowers from a beautiful garden.

Mrs. Farrell looked up, and saw Todd peering through the fence. "Hello!" she said. Todd was so scared, he couldn't move. Then Mrs. Farrell smiled. "Would you like to take some flowers with you?" she asked, walking toward the gate.

Todd knew that he shouldn't talk to strangers. He nodded his head, and she handed him a bright bouquet. "Thank you," he said, and then ran back to his bike and pedaled home as fast as he could.

When Todd handed the flowers to his mother, he told her what had happened. "I thought that Mrs. Farrell was a mean, scary old woman!" Todd said. "But she didn't seem so scary today."

"I'm sure she's a very nice lady," Todd's mother replied. "Should we invite her to our house for dessert? Sometimes, people aren't so frightening when you get to know them."

continued on page 163

Todd thought. "I'll make an invitation," he said.

He got out his best box of crayons and a piece of paper and drew a sunny picture with flowers. Inside, he wrote, "Please come to our house for dessert." His mother wrote their address inside, and Todd sealed the invitation in an envelope. Then he hopped on his bike, rode to Mrs. Farrell's house, put the note on the doorstep, rang the doorbell, and rode home.

At 7:00 o'clock that evening, there was a knock on the front door. Todd stood behind his father and mother as his mother opened the door. "Come in, Mrs. Farrell," his mother said. "I'm Lisa, this is my husband, Mark, and this is my son, Todd. Thank you for the lovely flowers!"

Mrs. Farrell held out her hand. "Pleased to meet you all," she said. "And call me Betsy. It's so nice to have someone call me by my name."

"Thank you for coming, Betsy," Todd's father replied.

"Todd and I baked brownies this afternoon. I hope you like chocolate!" Todd's mother said.

"My favorite!" Mrs. Farrell replied, as the four of them sat down at the kitchen table.

Mrs. Farrell told them all about her family. "My husband died three years ago, and I still miss him very much," she said. "My children are all grown and live far away, so I don't get to see my grandchildren very often. It's so nice to be with people! I get tired of having only myself to talk to. Thank you so much for inviting me over tonight."

"We are new to the neighborhood and don't know many other adults," Todd's mother replied. "We're so glad to have some company!"

When they finished the brownies and milk, Todd brought out his favorite book. "Would you read this to me?" he asked Mrs. Farrell.

"I'd be delighted!" she answered, and read Todd the book, not once, but three times.

The next day, Todd and his friend, Jay, were riding their bikes. They passed Mrs. Farrell's house. She happened to be walking to the mailbox.

"Look out! It's that scary old woman!" Jay shouted to Todd.

Todd stopped the bike, and got off. "Come on," he said to Jay. "I'd like you to meet my friend, Mrs. Farrell." ∎

Discussion Questions

1. Why were the children afraid of Mrs. Farrell?

2. When Mrs. Farrell gave Todd the flowers, did he do the right thing to go straight home and tell his parents? Why?

3. How do you think Mrs. Farrell felt when all the children stayed away from her?

4. Have you ever been scared of somebody you didn't know?

5. Name all the people in the story who made a new friend.

1, 2, 3 Activities!

The following activities will help reinforce the value of tolerance. Where appropriate, Activity Sheets can be duplicated for each child.

ACTIVITY 1—"WALK A MILE IN MY SHOES," p. 167

Supplies needed:

> Activity Sheet 1
> crayons
> pencils

Activity 1 is designed to let children take the place of someone else, to "walk in their shoes." It is helpful if you can invite people to visit the class, such as a person in a wheelchair, someone who is blind, or an older adult. They can each tell the children what it feels like to be "in their shoes."

If possible, have a wheelchair that the children can try sitting in. They can then feel how much harder it is to get in and out of a classroom, or elevator. Teach the children about the Braille system. Have an older adult talk about what he or she was like as a child, and how life was both the same and different, and how hard it is not to be as active as they once were.

Activity Sheet 1 can be used to write a thank-you note from the children to the class visitors.

ACTIVITY 2—"HOW DOES IT FEEL?" p. 168

Supplies needed:

> Activity Sheet 2
> pencils

Activity Sheet 2 allows children to examine pictures of different situations, and then to talk about how it might feel to be the person in the picture. The Activity Sheet begins with simple pictures: a girl on the beach, a boy eating a yummy ice cream sundae. The pictures display situations that are more and more uncomfortable. Let the children examine the pictures, and then ask the question, "How would it feel to be playing on the beach?" "How do you think the boy feels being the only child not chosen to play ball?" If the children are able to write, there is a space where they can write their answer. Share the answers with the whole group, and write them on the chalkboard or a large posterboard.

For the less comfortable situations, ask the children what they could do to make it better for the person. The more that the children are able to come up with appropriate answers, the more equipped they will be when confronted with actual situations.

ACTIVITY 3—"STICKS AND STONES," p. 169

Supplies needed:

Activity Sheet 3
large can
scissors
decorations for can
pencils

The old rhyme, "sticks and stones can break my bones, but names will never hurt me," is far from true. Children need to know that calling people cruel names or using words to hurt can be just as harmful as physical violence.

Using Activity Sheet 3, have the children cut out the pictures of the sticks and stones. Decorate a large can to display in the room. Call it the "Sticks and Stones Can." Whenever someone is caught calling someone else a name or saying something unkind, the teacher or parent writes the unkind word on one of the cutouts and places it in the can.

As the Sticks and Stones Can becomes full, talk to the children about how mean words add up to cause a lot of hurt. If the children can keep the can empty for a week, have a party to celebrate that they are now learning tolerance of others.

Tolerance

Walk a Mile in My Shoes

Dear _____

Thank you for coming to my class. I especially enjoyed

_____

_____

_____

_____

_____

_____

_____

_____

_____

_____

_____

_____

Sincerely,

_____

Tolerance

Name _____

How Does It Feel?

1

_____

2

_____

3

_____

4

_____

5

_____

6

_____

ACTIVITY SHEET 2

Tolerance

Sticks and Stones

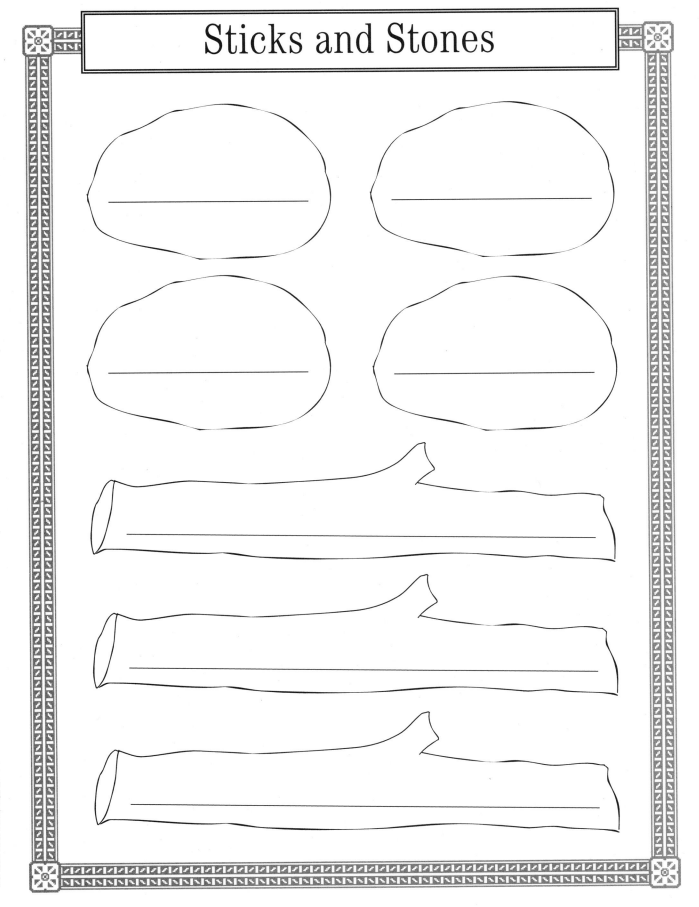

Community Connections

■ **Learn the history of your community.**

Discovering a "connecting point" among the various cultures in a community can help bring people together. Celebrating differences can also promote tolerance and respect.

Learn the history of your community. Who were the people who first settled in the area? Are there any people still living who remember what the landscape was like before houses were built? What historical archives are available?

A local librarian or historian could help. Check out the town hall, if there is one. As much as possible, try to use "human" resources—actual people who know the history and can help it come alive.

As a community learns its history and learns about the variety of people who made it possible, the community can learn to rejoice in the many people, past and present, who all share a "common-unity" with one another.

■ **Celebrate the ethnic variety of your community.**

Even if you live in a community that is not very diverse, there are a variety of ethnic and cultural heritages represented among the citizens. Through the school system or a civic society, plan a day of celebration, using the model of a street fair, carnival, or holiday gathering. All those who attend could be invited to wear clothing that represents their ancestral home, to fix traditional foods, and to teach crafts that tie in with their ethnic heritage.

■ **Volunteer to help with an agency such as a hospice.**

Does your community have a hospice or a similar organization that helps the sick, the poor, or the needy? Even children can make gifts or care packages to give to people who are critically ill or homeless. As adults and children work together to reach out to those who are less fortunate, there is less inclination to be critical or afraid of these people, and more likelihood of learning tolerance and compassion for other people.

■ Encourage the exchange of pen-pal letters.

Locate a nearby or faraway community where the cultural-ethnic makeup is different from your own community. Through local religious organizations, senior citizen groups, or "welcome wagons," an appeal can be made for pen-pal exchanges. Communicating with someone who lives in a different setting or who faces distinctive challenges from your own, can help you appreciate how other people live, thus enhancing a sincere tolerance for people of other backgrounds. You can exchange letters by post or by e-mail.

Reading List

The Christmas Menorahs: How a Town Fought Hate
by Janice Cohn

When a Jewish family is terrorized by threats and violence, a community joins together to show its solidarity against prejudice and racism.

Terrible Things
by Eve Bunting

The Terrible Things come to the forest and start removing all the animals, one group at a time, until only one, small rabbit is left. Little Rabbit realizes that if all the other animals had stuck together, they could have saved their community.

Hats Off to Hair!
by Virginia Kroll

With the use of rhyme and creative drawings, this book celebrates the varieties of hair and hairstyles that make each person unique.

My Head Is Full of Colors
by Catherine Friend

Maria discovers her own uniqueness, a recognition that allows each child to celebrate their diversity.

Ellis Island: Doorway to Freedom
by Steven Kroll

Young readers are given an introduction to America's continued attempt to be a place where all people can find a home, no matter where they come from.

Through Grandpa's Eyes
by Patricia MacLachlan

John learns how his blind grandpa "sees" the world. This story helps children understand that differences can make a person special, not strange.

continued on page 173

Talking to Angels
by Esther Watson

Through acceptance of her autistic sister, a little girl realizes how to accept and respect the differences in people.

Feathers and Fools
by Mem Fox

After a flock of swans and peacocks destroy each other, only two eggs are left: one, a peacock, and the other, a swan. When the eggs hatch, the two survivors choose to accept their differences, and live together in peace.

This Is Our House
by Michael Rosen

George won't allow anyone into his cardboard playhouse, but when the tables are turned, he learns a lesson about tolerance and accepting people no matter who they are.

Bear and Mrs. Duck
by P. Brewster

Although Bear and Mrs. Duck seem to have little in common, Bear finds out that variety can be fun.

Appendix

- **Group Projects**

- **Student Journal**

- **Miscellaneous Patterns**

- **Award Certificate**

- **About the Author**

Group Projects

Here are suggestions for ongoing group projects that give an overall view of the ten values, including:

1. A Tree of Values

2. A Living Rainbow

3. Hand-in-Hand Around the World

4. Wall of Fame

5. "WANTED" Posters

1.　A Tree of Values

Set aside a bulletin board or a portion of a wall to build a "value-able" tree, and then add to the "Tree of Values" each month.

Use the pattern sheet provided on p. 185. Gather a roll of brown paper, markers, and construction paper in a variety of colors.

a.　*Ten roots*

Cut from the roll of brown paper. Label each root is labeled with the name of one value.

b.　*A trunk.*

Cut from the roll of brown paper and label "Tree of Values" or "A Value-Able Tree."

c.　*Empty branches*

Cut from the roll of brown paper or large sheets of brown construction paper.

Trace and cut out the ten roots, and label each one with a different value: cooperation, courage, friendship, honesty, kindness, loyalty, respect, self-control, sharing, tolerance.

Trace and cut out the trunk. Staple it to a large bulletin board, or tape it to a door or wall of the room. There should be space for the branches to spread out and for the leaf-hands to be added throughout the year.

Trace and cut out the branches. Attach these to the top of the tree. Make sure to leave room for the leaf-hands to be added.

Script for Teacher/Group Leader:
"Look at this tree! It has a large trunk and many branches. What does the tree need to keep it rooted in the ground?

"The tree needs roots. Roots keep the tree firm and steady. Roots pull vitamins and water from the soil to feed the tree. Without roots, the tree could not live.

"I have ten roots to add to the tree. The roots have words on them. The words are the names of what we call *values*. What is a value? A value is something that makes us special. A value is something that helps us learn to be good, to take care of one another. Values help us live happy and healthy lives. Let's look at the names of the values on these roots." (Read off the names on each root, and then have the children place the roots on the tree.)

"The tree needs roots to live. But even with roots, the tree looks empty and bare. Wouldn't it look better if it were filled with leaves?

"You are going to help this tree fill with leaves! Every month, we are going to learn about one of the values, one of the roots on this tree. Each time we learn about a value, we're going to trace our handprint on a piece of colored paper and add it to the tree. By the end of the year, the tree will be filled with beautiful leaves."

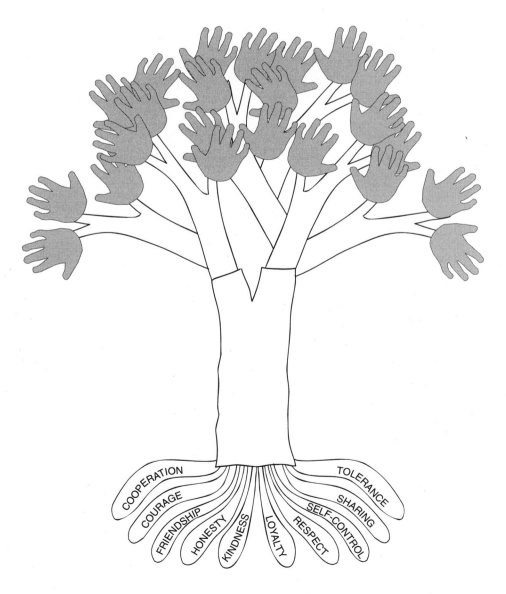

2. A Living Rainbow

For this project, find a large space (bulletin board, wall) on which to build a rainbow. Make a rainbow with all the colors of a real rainbow (red, orange, yellow, green, blue, indigo, violet), plus black (background), white (clouds), and brown (ground).

Begin with black for the background. Have each child trace his or her hand on a piece of black construction paper and cut out the hand. On the black paper hand, using white crayon, have the child write his or her name and the first value, cooperation. Staple the hands on the bulletin board or wall set aside for the completed rainbow.

During Chapter 2, use brown construction paper and have the children trace one of their hands. Ask them to write their name and the name of the second value, courage, on their brown paper hand. Staple the brown hands on the bottom of the bulletin board to represent the firm ground we build our values on.

In Chapter 3, the value is friendship. Following the same procedure, the children will make hands out of violet (or dark purple) construction paper. Staple the hands on top of the black background and above the ground in an arch shape, to create the base of the rainbow.

How to Build a Rainbow

STEP 10: Add white hand prints (*tolerance*) to the sky to form clouds. →

STEP 3-9: Build the arches of the rainbow from the ground up. Each arch is a different color and represents a different value. →

STEP 1: Create a black background with black hand prints (*cooperation*). ↓

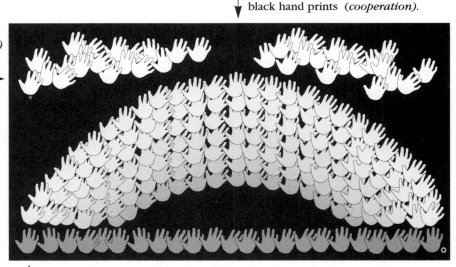

↑ **STEP 2:** Add brown hand prints (*courage*) to form the ground.

As the children learn a new value, they will repeat this process. Each value is a separate color. The handprints are stapled to the bulletin board in an arch, so that a rainbow is built.

Say to the children, "See how bright and beautiful the world is when we all practice these values!"

The colors for each value:

COOPERATION: . . . . Black *(background)*

COURAGE: . . . . Brown *(firm ground)*

FRIENDSHIP: . . . . Violet *(dark purple)*

HONESTY: . . . . Indigo *(light purple)*

KINDNESS: . . . . Blue

LOYALTY: . . . . Green

RESPECT: . . . . Yellow

SELF-CONTROL: . . . . Orange

SHARING: . . . . Red

TOLERANCE: . . . . White *(clouds)*

3.   Hand-in-Hand Around the World

When a lesson on a particular value is completed, have each child draw his or her handprint on a piece of paper. Each child then writes the name of the value and his or her own name on the paper hand. The hands are taped on the wall, one after the next, to form a long chain. The idea is to join hands around the world, working together to be value-able people. You may use the same color for all values or use the color guide for the project on p. 179.

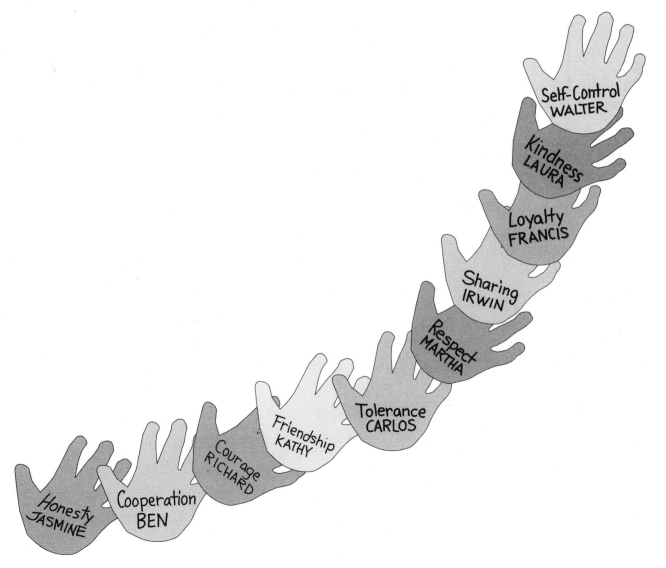

4. Wall of Fame

Designate a space in the room for a "Wall of Fame." Place this title in large letters in the designated space.

Using the star pattern below, photocopy a collection of stars in various colors and cut them out. On each star write "_____ is a star at _____." Then every time a child exhibits one of the values in a special way (sharing with a new student, telling the truth, etc.), fill out a star. "Joseph is a star at being kind," for example. Then place the star on the Wall of Fame and praise the child for living out the value.

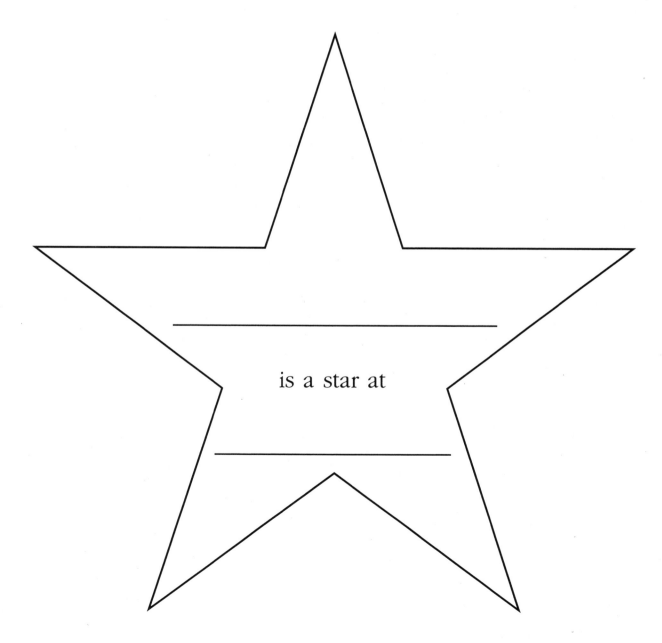

is a star at

5. WANTED Posters

Create a poster for each value using posterboard. At the top of each poster in bold letters write "WANTED," and under this space write the name of a value, again in bold letters. Beneath this make a listing of characteristics intrinsic to that value (have the children help with the definitions). At the bottom of the poster write, "REWARD: The joy of knowing that your kindness (or whatever value is listed) has made this world a better place" (or ". . . has made someone's life a little brighter," etc.).

As children model kindness, their name is written on the poster provided.

WANTED
Kindness

Looking for people with the following characteristics:

_____

_____

_____

_____

_____

_____

_____

_____

REWARD: The joy of knowing that your kindness has made this world a better place.

_____   _____   _____

_____   _____   _____

_____   _____   _____

Student Journal

Each child can create his or her own journal using activity sheets included in each lesson on values. The journal begins with a title page, see page 184, telling about the child (the "author" of the journal).

To create a journal portfolio, give children a separate manila file folder and let them label it with their names and then decorate it. Assist children with their names if necessary. The folder is used to collect the completed activity sheets for each month. At the end of the year, have each child design a cover page and then have it laminated. Bind the pages together, creating a lasting Journal of Values for each child to keep.

I AM A VALUE-ABLE PERSON!
My Journal of Values

Author's name (me): _____

I am _____ years old.

My birthday is _____.

My address is _____.

I am _____ inches tall.

My favorite color is_____.

My favorite food is _____.

My favorite book is _____.

I am special because_____

_____

_____.

There's nobody else like me!

Miscellaneous Patterns

Tree of Values

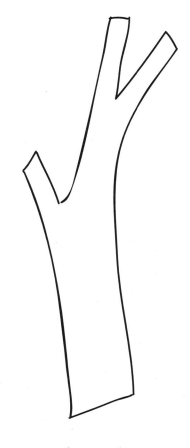

branch

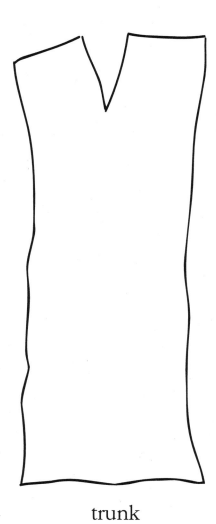

trunk

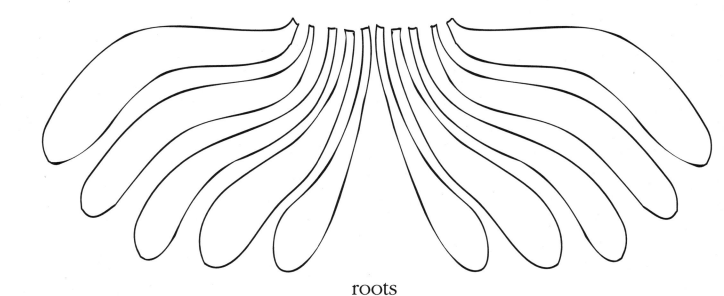

roots

Award Certificate

Cooperation Courage

Friendship Honesty

Tolerance

Sharing

Self-Control

Kindness

_____

(name)

is a Value-Able person!

Respect Loyalty

About the Author

Kathleen Long Bostrom is an author, a Presbyterian minister, and a parent. She has a Bachelor of Arts degree in Psychology from California State University, Long Beach, California, and a Master of Arts in Christian Education and a Master of Divinity degree from Princeton Theological Seminary, New Jersey. She will graduate with a Doctor of Ministry in Preaching from McCormick Theological Seminary in June 2000.

Kathy is an award-winning preacher and has published a number of sermons and articles. Her first children's picture book, *The World That God Made,* was published in September 1997. Her series of books for young children, "Questions from Little Hearts," debuted in March 1998 with *What Is God Like?*. Book two in the series, *Who*

Is Jesus? is planned for publication in February 1999. She has a number of other books under contract.

Kathy and her husband, Greg, serve as co-pastors of the Wildwood Presbyterian Church near Chicago, Illinois. Kathy and Greg have three children: Christopher, Amy, and David. The author is an avid reader and enjoys collecting children's books, walking, and spending time with her family.